SCHILLEBEECKX

OUTSTANDING CHRISTIAN THINKERS

Series Editor: Brian Davies OP

The series offers a range of authoritative studies on people who have made an outstanding contribution to Christian thought and understanding. The series will range across the full spectrum of Christian thought to include Catholic and Protestant thinkers, to cover East and West, historical and contemporary figures. By and large, each volume will focus on a single 'thinker', but occasionally the subject may be a movement or a school of thought.

Brian Davies OP, the Series Editor, is Regent of Studies at Blackfriars, Oxford, where he also teaches philosophy. He is a member of the Theology Faculty at the University of Oxford and tutor at St Benet's Hall, Oxford. He has lectured regularly at the University of Bristol, Fordham University, New York, and the Beda College, Rome. He is Reviews Editor of *New Blackfriars*. His previous publications include: *An Introduction to the Philosophy of Religion* (OUP, 1982); *Thinking about God* (Geoffrey Chapman, 1985); *The Thought of Thomas Aquinas* (OUP, 1992); and he was editor of *Language, Meaning and God* (Geoffrey Chapman, 1987).

Already published:

The Apostolic Fathers
Simon Tugwell OP

Denys the Areopagite
Andrew Louth

The Venerable Bede
Benedicta Ward SLG

Anselm
G.R. Evans

Teresa of Avila
Rowan Williams

Handel
Hamish Swanston

Jonathan Edwards
John E. Smith

Bultmann
David Fergusson

Reinhold Niebuhr
Kenneth Durkin

Karl Rahner
William V. Dych SJ

Lonergan
Frederick E. Crowe SJ

Hans Urs von Balthasar
John O'Donnell SJ

Yves Congar
Aidan Nichols OP

Schillebeeckx
Philip Kennedy OP

Planned titles in the series include:

The Cappadocians
Anthony Meredith SJ

SCHILLEBEECKX

Philip Kennedy OP

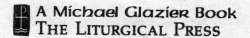
A Michael Glazier Book
THE LITURGICAL PRESS

A Michael Glazier Book
published by The Liturgical Press
St John's Abbey, Collegeville, MN 56321, USA

Published in Great Britain by Geoffrey Chapman, a Cassell imprint

First published 1993

Library of Congress Cataloging-in-Publication Data
A catalog record for this book is available from the Library of Congress.

ISBN 0-8146-5502-5

Typeset by Colset Private Limited, Singapore
Printed and bound in Great Britain by
Biddles Ltd, Guildford and King's Lynn

Contents

*To the Community of the
Albertinum in Nijmegen*

and in memory of

*Gerald Daily (1927–77)
Desmond O'Connor (1909–88)
and Edward Stormon (1912–92)
of the Society of Jesus*

Editorial foreword

St Anselm of Canterbury once described himself as someone with faith seeking understanding. In words addressed to God he says 'I long to understand in some degree thy truth, which my heart believes and loves. For I do not seek to understand that I may believe, but I believe in order to understand.'

And this is what Christians have always inevitably said, either explicitly or implicitly. Christianity rests on faith, but it also has content. It teaches and proclaims a distinctive and challenging view of reality. It naturally encourages reflection. It is something to think about; something about which one might even have second thoughts.

But what have the greatest Christian thinkers said? And is it worth saying? Does it engage with modern problems? Does it provide us with a vision to live by? Does it make sense? Can it be preached? Is it believable?

This series originates with questions like these in mind. Written by experts, it aims to provide clear, authoritative and critical accounts of outstanding Christian writers from New Testament times to the present. It will range across the full spectrum of Christian thought to include Catholic and Protestant thinkers, thinkers from East and West, thinkers ancient, mediaeval and modern.

The series draws on the best scholarship currently available, so it will interest all with a professional concern for the history of Christian ideas. But contributors will also be writing for general readers who have little or no previous knowledge of the subjects to be dealt with. Volumes to appear should therefore prove helpful at a popular as well as an academic level. For the most part they will be devoted to a single thinker, but occasionally the subject will be a movement or school of thought.

The present volume, devoted to the Belgian author Fr Edward Schillebeeckx OP, is designed as a guide to the large and complex body of work of one of the most influential and controversial of modern theologians. Schillebeeckx's career has spanned most of the twentieth century, so the book explains his constantly evolving thought against the backdrop of developments in twentieth-century philosophy and theology. It is especially concerned to show that the key to understanding Schillebeeckx lies in his view of God as Creator and in his view of Jesus of Nazareth as the manifestation of everything involved in creation.

Schillebeeckx has become especially well known for his writings on Jesus and on ministry. This book traces his thoughts on these matters, but it also highlights his way of explaining how, and in what sense, human beings know God the Creator. In doing so, it draws attention to the most interesting and original feature of Schillebeeckx's thought: his account of the meaning of faith in God in cultural contexts where faith is regarded as meaningless.

The work of Edward Schillebeeckx is an essential subject of study for anyone with a serious interest in modern theology. This book is the first comprehensive and authoritative account of the range of his writings to appear in English. Like other volumes in the *Outstanding Christian Thinkers* series, it is written with an eye on non-professional readers. But it will also be much welcomed by teachers of theology and professional theologians. It is based on lengthy study of Schillebeeckx's published works in the language in which they were written. It also draws on significant archival material concerning his lecture notes hitherto unused in English studies of his thought.

Philip Kennedy OP has studied the thinking of Schillebeeckx with supervision from Schillebeeckx himself. I am delighted to say that Fr Schillebeeckx has read the following text with approval and has kindly agreed to write a note to accompany it.

Brian Davies OP

Foreword

In this book, Philip Kennedy tries, in a straightforward, clear, but theologically sound way, to make the philosophical, ethical and theological significance of my theological publications accessible to a large reading public. In doing so, he presents my theology as 'a mirror of twenty centuries of theological history' — which is quite something, although I must admit that 'the great Catholic traditions', from the Bible to the present day, in confrontation with contemporary personal and collective experiences, have always seemed to me to be the appropriate field of activity for the theologian. I have indeed learnt to detest rigid thinking and empty speculation because they manipulate reality: they are not true to what presents itself to us as day-to-day reality.

What makes Kennedy's book special is that it not only analyses the main themes of my theology but also provides the reader with a living 'biography'. It presents the reader with a picture of the life of the theologian he is studying, so that he does not have to try and imagine an 'abstract person' without a context. In addition to an account of the theologian's thought, the reader is also given the theologian's photograph as a bonus, so to speak. Many readers will find this a point in the book's favour.

The author also shows a special interest in the sources of my thinking. All thinkers, even if they should occasionally transcend the boundaries of their time, will nevertheless always remain children of their time, influenced by many different, specific and unspecific, concrete and vague events and impressions, in ways that cannot always be deciphered or traced back. They are affected by their environment just as they, in their turn, also have an effect on their environment. I was not a little surprised to read that the author has discovered traces of the influence of eighteen different schools of thought in my theological publications. While reading the following book, I thought to myself that sometimes ordinary everyday occurrences in my life may very well have influenced my thinking more profoundly than some school of thought that I have studied and subsequently mentioned in the critical apparatus of my books or articles. An eager susceptibility to everything 'outside' and an openness to everything that has the power to sensitize one provide so many conscious — and perhaps even more unconscious — impressions and stimuli that influence one's thought. So a catalogue of influences (based on texts and quotations) will of necessity always be inadequate and fail to do justice to more indefinable, and less easily identifiable influences that one has assimilated. The author cannot be blamed for this. I am aware of the fact that, for instance, the two long years I spent studying Structuralism have introduced an element of restraint and caution in my hermeneutically actualizing and critical thinking in some respects. But on the whole they have hardly influenced or changed my theological views at all (although I do not in the least regret having spent time on this — for me — difficult subject).

The study of sources remains a precarious and always selective undertaking. I admire the way in which Philip Kennedy has rendered the basic intentions of my theological project, as well as the main themes, as I see them, of a systematic theology based on history and with experience as its critical reference point, in such a lucid, readable and yet precise way in the eight chapters of this book.

The only thing that is lacking is a separate chapter on eschatology, which (together with theology and its epistemological implications — creation, Christology and the sacraments) is one of the fundamental focal points of my theological quest, although I admit that most of the available material on the subject (and accessible to the author) has not been published. I welcome all criticism except when it is unfounded. That is why I am very grateful to the author because, after years of study, he (in contrast to a recent author from Louvain, who casually and, to my mind, incomprehensibly, reproaches me with having a 'dualistic world view') concludes that 'The manner in which Schillebeeckx speaks about creation reveals him as a markedly anti-dualist and anti-supernaturalist thinker' (p. 93).

I expect that we will be hearing more from Philip Kennedy. I hope that he will regard this Foreword as an encouragement from an older colleague who is putting down his pen to let others speak — an encouragement for a younger, committed fellow theologian starting out on the laborious task of making the liberating gospel of Jesus Christ accessible to people in need of spiritual welfare in a way that is both true to the gospel and (in these early 'postmodern' days) understandable. Believers are craving for a meaningful theology.

Dear Philip, take that from an old colleague in the field.

Edward Schillebeeckx
Nijmegen,
15 December 1992

Preface

I left Australia in the middle of 1986 to study theology in Europe. I completed this book when I returned to Melbourne. My studies abroad were based in Switzerland, but they led me several times to visit the Dominicans of Nijmegen in the Netherlands, among whom I had the privilege to meet Professor Edward Schillebeeckx. During subsequent visits and, for me, difficult years of study, he readily gave of his time and resources to assist my work; as did his community in the Albertinum. I should like to record my profound thanks to him, to the Dutch Dominicans, and to all the members of his community; in particular, to Ted Schoof OP, of Nijmegen's Faculty of Theology. I am grateful, as well, to my Dutch tutor in Nijmegen, Hermein Jansen, to Dr Meeuwes Pool, and for conversations with the Dutch theologian Dr Erik Borgman.

My interpretation of Schillebeeckx's work has been aided considerably over recent years by Professor Guido Vergauwen OP, of the University of Fribourg, in Switzerland. I thank him for his unflagging readiness to offer advice and for his critical eye. I am also most appreciative for the friendly support of Angel Maestro OP of Madrid; the Revd Margaret Mascall of the Archdiocese of Canterbury; Vicente Botella OP, of Valencia; Dr John Paul Mahoney OP, of Providence College, USA; Dr Kenneth Parker of Saint Louis University; Dr Gerard Norton OP in Dublin; and in Switzerland, Patrick and Ruth O'Laoghaire-Doblies, Helga and Willy Kaufman, Yvan Mudry, Roberto Simona, and the Dominican friars of Fribourg.

I was able to spend such a long time away from my country because of the generous support of my family in Australia and the Dominicans of my Province. I am sincerely mindful of the sacrifices made to enable me to study full-time over several years.

The fact that I began this book in Switzerland – after completing a doctoral dissertation – and finished it in Australia might well have tested the patience of both my publisher and editor, as I moved from continent to continent. I am entirely grateful, therefore, to the publishers, Geoffrey Chapman, for discreetly waiting for me to settle back in Australia, and to my editor, Brian Davies OP, for a similar forbearance coupled with his most incisive and constructive criticism and suggestions.

Where error or contentious conclusion remains in this work, I should point out that I am entirely to blame, and hope that others will improve my thoughts.

Philip Kennedy OP
Saint Dominic's Priory
Melbourne
3 November 1992

Select bibliography

Works

An extensive bibliography of the works of Schillebeeckx until 1983 is available in Robert J. Schreiter (ed.), *The Schillebeeckx Reader* (New York: Crossroad, 1984; Edinburgh: T. & T. Clark, 1986), pp. 297–321. The following publications are referred to in the course of this study. Titles are listed chronologically with details of republication and English translation where applicable.

De Sacramentele Heilseconomie: Theologische bezinning op S. Thomas' sacramentenleer in het licht van de traditie en van de hedendaagse sacramentsproblematiek (Antwerp: H. Nelissen, 1952).

Maria, moeder van de verlossing (Antwerp/Haarlem: Apostolaat van de Rosenkrans, 1955); *Mary, Mother of the Redemption* (London: Sheed & Ward, 1964/1983).

Op zoek naar de levende God (Utrecht and Nijmegen: Dekker & Van de Vegt, 1958).

Christus sacrament van de Godsontmoeting (Bilthoven: H. Nelissen, 1959/1966); *Christ the Sacrament of the Encounter with God* (London: Sheed & Ward, 1963/1985).

Het huwelijk: aardse werkelijkheid en heilsmysterie (Bilthoven: H. Nelissen, 1963), I; *Marriage: Human Reality and Saving Mystery* (London: Sheed & Ward, 1965/1984).

Openbaring en Theologie, 2nd edn (*Theologische Peilingen*, I; Bilthoven: H. Nelissen, 1964); *Revelation and Theology*, 1: *Revelation, Tradition and Theological Reflection* (London: Sheed & Ward, 1967/1987); *Revelation and Theology*, 2: *The Concept of Truth and Theological Renewal* (London: Sheed & Ward, 1968/1987).

God en Mens (*Theologische Peilingen*, II; Bilthoven: H. Nelissen, 1965); *God and Man* (London: Sheed & Ward, 1969/1979).

Het ambts-celibaat in de branding: een kritische bezinning
(Bilthoven: H. Nelissen, 1966); *Clerical Celibacy Under Fire: A
Critical Appraisal*, trans. C. A. L. Jarrott (London and Sydney,
Sheed & Ward, 1968).

Het tweede Vaticaans Concilie (Bilthoven: H. Nelissen, 1966);
Vatican II: The Real Achievement (London and Melbourne:
Sheed & Ward, 1967).

Wereld en Kerk (Theologische Peilingen, III; Bilthoven: H. Nelissen,
1966); *World and Church* (London: Sheed & Ward, 1971/1983).

Christus' tegenwoordigheid in de eucharistie (Bilthoven: H.
Nelissen, 1967); *The Eucharist* (London: Sheed & Ward,
1968/1983).

Zending van de Kerk (Theologische Peilingen, IV; Bilthoven: H.
Nelissen, 1968); *The Mission of the Church* (London: Sheed &
Ward, 1973/1981).

God the Future of Man (London and Sydney: Sheed & Ward,
1969/1986); no Dutch original as a book.

Geloofsverstaan: interpretatie en kritiek (Theologische Peilingen,
V; Bloemendaal: H. Nelissen, 1972); *The Understanding of
Faith: Interpretation and Criticism* (London: Sheed & Ward,
1974/1981).

Jezus, het verhaal van een levende (Brugge and Bloemendaal: H.
Nelissen, 1974); *Jesus: An Experiment in Christology*, trans.
Hubert Hoskins (New York: Seabury, 1979/London: Collins,
1979/New York: Crossroad, 1981).

Gerechtigheid en liefde: Genade en bevrijding, 2nd edn (Baarn: H.
Nelissen, 1977); *Christ: The Christian Experience in the Modern
World*, trans. John Bowden (London: SCM, 1980).

Tussentijds verhaal over twee Jezus boeken (Bloemendaal: H.
Nelissen, 1978); *Interim Report on the Books 'Jesus' and 'Christ'*,
trans. John Bowden (London: SCM, 1980).

Kerkelijk ambt: Voorgangers in de gemeente van Jezus Christus,
2nd edn (Bloemendaal: H. Nelissen, 1980); *Ministry: A Case for
Change*, trans. John Bowden (London: SCM, 1981/1984).

Evangelie verhalen (Baarn: H. Nelissen, 1982); *God Among Us: The
Gospel Proclaimed*, trans. John Bowden (New York: Crossroad,
1983).

In conversation with Huub Oosterhuis and Piet Hoogeveen, *God is
ieder ogenblik nieuw: Gesprekken met Edward Schillebeeckx*
(Baarn: Amboboeken, 1982); *God Is New Each Moment*, trans.
David Smith (Edinburgh: T. & T. Clark, 1983).

Theologisch Geloofsverstaan Anno 1983 (Baarn: H. Nelissen,
1983).

Robert J. Schreiter (ed.), *The Schillebeeckx Reader* (New York:
Crossroad, 1984; Edinburgh: T. & T. Clark, 1986).

*Pleidooi voor mensen in de kerk: christelijke identiteit en ambten in
de kerk* (Baarn: H. Nelissen, 1985); *The Church with a Human
Face: A New and Expanded Theology of Ministry*, trans. John
Bowden (London: SCM, 1985).

Als politiek niet alles is: Jezus in de westerse cultuur (Baarn: Ten

Have, 1986); *Jesus in Our Western Culture: Mysticism, Ethics and Politics*, trans. John Bowden (London: SCM, 1987).

Om het behoud van het evangelie (*Evangelie verhalen*, II; Baarn: H. Nelissen, 1988); *For the Sake of the Gospel*, trans. John Bowden (London: SCM, 1989).

Een democratische kerk (Nijmegen: De Bazuin, 1989).

Mensen als verhaal van God, 1st edn (Baarn: H. Nelissen, 1989); 2nd edn (Baarn, 1990); *Church: The Human Story of God*, trans. John Bowden (London: SCM, 1990).

Further reading

John Bowden, *Edward Schillebeeckx: Portrait of a Theologian* (London: SCM, 1983).

Louis Dupré, 'Experience and interpretation: a philosophical reflection on Schillebeeckx' Jesus and Christ', *Theological Studies* 43 (1982), pp. 30–51.

Peter Hebblethwaite, *The New Inquisition? The Case of Edward Schillebeeckx and Hans Küng* (San Francisco: Harper & Row, 1980).

Mary Catherine Hilkert, 'Hermeneutics of history in the theology of Edward Schillebeeckx', *Thomist* 51 (1987), pp. 97–145.

Fergus Kerr, 'Edward Schillebeeckx' in Alan Bullock and R. B. Woodings (eds), *The Fontana Dictionary of Modern Thinkers* (London: Fontana, 1983), pp. 680–1.

Yvan Mudry, 'Edward Schillebeeckx: L'église face au monde', *Choisir* (April 1989), pp. 12–15.

John Nijenhuis, 'Christology without Jesus of Nazareth is ideology: a monumental work by Schillebeeckx on Jesus', *Journal of Ecumenical Studies* 17 (1980), pp. 125–40.

William L. Portier, 'Edward Schillebeeckx as critical theorist: the impact of neo-Marxist social thought on his recent theology', *Thomist* 48 (1984), pp. 341–67.

'Schillebeeckx' dialogue with critical theory', *Ecumenist* 21 (1983), pp. 20–7.

Mark [= Ted] Schoof, 'Dutch Catholic theology: a new approach to Christology', *Cross Currents* 22 (1973), pp. 415–27.

'Masters in Israel: VII. The later theology of Edward Schillebeeckx', *Clergy Review* 55:12 (1970), pp. 943–60.

(ed.), *The Schillebeeckx Case: Official Exchange of Letters and Documents in the Investigation of Fr. Edward Schillebeeckx by the Sacred Congregation for the Doctrine of the Faith, 1976–1980* (New York/Ramsey, NJ: Paulist Press, 1984).

'E. Schillebeeckx: 25 years in Nijmegen', *Theology Digest* 37 (1990), pp. 313–32; 38 (1991), pp. 31–44.

Robert J. Schreiter, 'Edward Schillebeeckx' in Martin E. Marty and Dean G. Peermen (eds), *A Handbook of Christian Theologians*, enlarged edn (Nashville: Abingdon, 1987), pp. 625–38.

'Edward Schillebeeckx' in David F. Ford (ed.), *The Modern*

Theologians: An Introduction to Christian Theology in the Twen-
tieth Century, 2 vols (Oxford: Basil Blackwell, 1989), I,
pp. 152–63.
(ed.) 'Edward Schillebeeckx: an orientation to his thought' in *The*
Schillebeeckx Reader (New York: Crossroad, 1984), pp. 1–24.
Robert J. Schreiter and Mary Catherine Hilkert (eds), *The Praxis of*
Christian Experience: An Introduction to the Theology of
Edward Schillebeeckx (San Francisco: Harper & Row, 1989).
Leonard Swidler and Piet F. Fransen (eds), *Authority in the Church*
and the Schillebeeckx Case (New York: Crossroad, 1982).

Abbreviations

CHF	*The Church with a Human Face: A New and Expanded Theology of Ministry*
CS	*Christ the Sacrament of the Encounter with God*
FSG	*For the Sake of the Gospel*
GAU	*God Among Us: The Gospel Proclaimed*
GFM	*God the Future of Man*
GM	*God and Man*
GNM	*God is New Each Moment*
IR	*Interim Report on the Books 'Jesus' and 'Christ'*
JWC	*Jesus in Our Western Culture: Mysticism, Ethics and Politics*
M	*Mary, Mother of the Redemption*
MC	*The Mission of the Church*
Min	*Ministry: A Case for Change*
RT1	*Revelation and Theology, 1: Revelation, Tradition and Theological Reflection*
RT2	*Revelation and Theology, 2: The Concept of Truth and Theological Renewal*
SC	Ted Schoof (ed.), *The Schillebeeckx Case*
UF	*The Understanding of Faith: Interpretation and Criticism*
WC	*World and Church*
I	*Jesus: An Experiment in Christology*
II	*Christ: The Christian Experience in the Modern World*
III	*Church: The Human Story of God*

Full details of these works are cited in the Bibliography.

1

Coming to grips with Schillebeeckx

This book describes the life and work of the twentieth-century Belgian theologian Edward Schillebeeckx. It attempts to explain why he is an outstanding Christian thinker and provides an interpretation of the essential features of his theology. In so doing it concentrates less on his person and more on the life-long endeavour to which he has devoted his time, talents, and energies. That endeavour has amounted to nothing less than a quest sustained over several decades to explain what Christian faith in God and Jesus Christ might mean.The consuming and overriding enthusiasm of Schillebeeckx's life has been to elucidate the sense of Christian faith in cultural contexts in which religious faith is upbraided as meaningless, or worse, as an outright impediment to human development and freedom. This opening chapter confines itself to fairly general remarks concerning Schillebeeckx's thought. Subsequent chapters will probe his achievements in greater detail and occasionally discuss more debatable aspects of his publications.

SOME DISCONCERTING TRAITS

We may take it well and truly for granted that Schillebeeckx is a difficult theologian to follow. Even his name is somewhat off-putting on first hearing. Other disconcerting factors frustrating initial efforts to come to grips with the nature and significance of his thought are even more daunting and can be mentioned briefly as follows.

To begin with, Schillebeeckx has published a vast amount of material during his career: about five hundred books and articles issued over the past five decades.[1] Almost all of these were originally written in Dutch and a good many have never been translated. Even so, most of them have been translated at some stage into languages such as English, Spanish, Italian, German, French, and Japanese, to name but a few. For someone who has neither heard of nor read Schillebeeckx, the voluminousness of his works could easily prove too bewildering to stimulate interest in his arguments.

In addition, Schillebeeckx has spent nearly all of his life in the north-western corner of Europe. He has been a professor of theology for over forty years, a Catholic priest for more than fifty, and a Dominican friar for nearly sixty. An unfamiliarity with the intellectual and cultural history of Belgium and the Netherlands, or with the quite specific theological traditions that have marked his life, could also frustrate an attempt to become conversant with his work.

Thirdly, Schillebeeckx has spent the greater part of his life labouring and lecturing in universities. Thousands of pages of his lecture notes have been catalogued in Dutch and Belgian archives without ever having been published. These largely inaccessible notes contain valuable clues for comprehending the characteristics and development of his theology, but they are of little use for anyone who has no access to the archives housed in the cities where he taught.

Fourthly, it could hardly be over-emphasized for the English-speaking reader of Schillebeeckx's work that many Europeans of his type and age were steeped in a knowledge of philosophical writings since their adolescent days at school. All of which is to say that his writings are informed by a broad knowledge both of the history of Western philosophy and of European philosophical developments peculiar to the twentieth century. To penetrate his thought it is necessary to fathom the philosophical issues suffusing his theological studies. It is also needful to discern what he intends by the philosophical terminology he uses. His writings abound with philosophical expressions like 'contingency', 'praxis', and 'universality'. And yet, terms such as these are more often than not given merely laconic definitions in his publications.

Another reason why Schillebeeckx is occasionally held at arm's length is because he is described at times as a controversial theologian. Controversial, that is, in the sense of being judged as somewhat out of step with officially sanctioned schools of thought in the church of his own confession—the Roman Catholic Church. It is not uncommon to find him grouped with people like Hans Küng, Leonardo Boff, Charles Curran, and Matthew Fox (all quite different contemporary Roman Catholic theologians) as a betrayer of tradition and a corruptor of faith.[2] I hope to show that to describe Schillebeeckx as standing outside a mainstream of traditional Christian thought and practice is seriously to mischaracterize him. One might well take issue with many of his theological and philosophical assumptions, and in this book his work will at times be criticized constructively as well as expounded, but I would still commend the view that he is a profoundly traditional and Catholic thinker.

A sixth reason why his theology may prove baffling has to do with a matter of change. To read his publications in chronological sequence is to become aware of a prominent metamorphosis at the heart of his work. His later writings are clearly distinguishable from his first essays in terms of themes, terminology, method, and philosophical argumentation. For example, his early writings discuss the family rosary and Roman Catholic sacraments, whereas his latest articles debate biological engineering and ecological despolation. His first works extol Mary, the mother of Jesus, though little is said of her in his recent studies.[3] In his initial publications he talks about God and Christ in the context of Church and sacrament. His latter-day publications speak of God and Jesus in categories of politics and suffering. How is this change to be explained? Has Schillebeeckx radically altered his theological style just as Stravinsky occasionally changed substantially his compositional method? If a substantive change is detectable in Schillebeeckx's theology, then who or what instigated it? In short, a readily discernible intellectual evolution in his publications complicates the issue of locating the intellectual pivots upon which he builds his theology.

In the seventh place, Schillebeeckx's writings can give the impression of being arcane and eclectic because they draw from a large multilingual pool of ancient, biblical, mediaeval, modern and contemporary texts. His works are wont to cite philosophical, sociological, and political studies of an uncompromising difficulty. His own ability to read and work in many different languages, ancient and modern, and his familiarity with writings of considerable complexity, have contributed to his readiness to use highly technical language. He once spoke, for example, of semiotics and dissymmetrical isotopes in an article issued for public consideration.[4]

UNDERSTANDING SCHILLEBEECKX

The disconcerting traits of Schillebeeckx's work thus described render the task of comprehending his theology appreciably more complex, but they should not be overplayed. His output is not a hermetic, impenetrable collection of esoteric texts. Ironically, coming to grips with the essentials of his theology becomes a remarkably straightforward affair once a few of the pillars of his thought have been spotlighted. His work is of a piece in that his theology's most basic conceptual infrastructure has never changed substantially during the full length of his career. He has consistently held a single intellectual problem sharply in focus throughout his multifarious publications; and his superintending intellectual and religious interests can be outlined briefly and plainly.

The problem he has persistently held at the centre of his attention is the most nettlesome dilemma confronting the discipline of theology. The problem is not new and was well known to Aristotle

(384–322 BCE). It is the quandary of explaining how that which is absolute, called God, or Allah, in the context of religion, can be recognized and contacted in that which is limited, localized, historical, and particular. For Schillebeeckx, theology is a matter of describing how the absolute is unveiled, so to speak, in the relative; the ultimate in the limited (see GAU, p. 157).[5]

Philosophically expressed, his works seek to unravel the interplay between universality and particularity. Theologically worded, his publications are impelled from beginning to end by the task of explaining the mediation of divine transcendence in human, historical immanence. Christologically stated (that is, in the context of interpreting the ultimate identity and significance of Jesus Christ), Schillebeeckx is bent on clarifying the meaning, and justifying the truth, of the Christian profession that a man of antiquity, Jesus of Nazareth, and a man executed as a criminal at that, was and is the pre-eminent manifestation of God for all people at all times. Whatever the theological topic expounded by Schillebeeckx in his writings, one philosophical conundrum overrides all others in his expositions — the conundrum involved in the assertion that universality can be located in particularity.

The same problem is ever-present in ethical enquiries under the form of the question as to whether ethical norms should be regarded as variable human artifacts or as absolutely and immutably prescriptive in value.

The universality/particularity theme running through Schillebeeckx's studies has become uppermost in present-day theological discussions concerning encounters between the world's religions.[6] Schillebeeckx is an outstanding Christian thinker because he has been able to explain the uniqueness and universal relevance of Christian faith without unjustifiably discriminating against the intrinsic worth of other religions (religious exclusivism); or by subsuming the value of all religions under the umbrella of Christianity's worth (inclusivism); or, finally, by maintaining that all religions are of equal import (universalism) (see III, pp. 159–86).

Despite its complexity, therefore, there is much to be gleaned from a study of Schillebeeckx's thought as it is expressed in his writings. My overarching aim in this book is twofold: to provide a ready access to the pivotal features of his thought, and to illustrate his pre-eminence as a Christian thinker. In all that follows I propose to lay bare the essentials of his theology as I understand them. But by speaking of 'Schillebeeckx's theology' in this book, I am not suggesting that his work is purely the fruit of his own intelligence and inventiveness. His evident originality notwithstanding, it is as well to recognize that his theology is heir to a long ancestry of Christian reflection. With his multifaceted body of writings he effectively unfolds his own formulation and reinterpretation of traditional currents of Christian theology. His theology is in the first instance a version, revision, and recasting of Christian theology. He may be regarded as an outstanding Christian thinker precisely because his works mirror twenty centuries of reflection on Christian belief. To read his publications is to be confronted by a compendium of two millennia of theological history. Nearly every major theological theme elaborated in his works is traceable either in biblical texts or in the writings of traditional Christian thinkers. He quite self-consciously acknowledges his debt to what he calls 'the great Christian tradition' (III, p. 15). The point to be stressed here is that Schillebeeckx enunciates his theology in concert with other Christian thinkers. His importance as a Christian thinker does not reside merely in a powerful theological originality or daring inventiveness. It lies primarily in his wide-ranging familiarity with biblical and post-biblical Christian traditions, and particularly with the Dominican tradition that he has made his own.

He is also a resolutely ecumenical theologian who examines and debates the theological inquiries of many different Christian churches. More than that, quite apart from taking into account the quite literally scandalous divisions between Christian denominations, his later work concentrates on a much more unsettling ecumenical divorce, namely, the ever-present and ubiquitous economic and political chasm between people who are well-off and those who are destitute (GAU, p. 178).

What is more, Edward Schillebeeckx is most decidedly a Dominican theologian. His theological preoccupations have been directly moulded by his day-to-day life as a Dominican friar. One example will serve here to underscore his Dominican cast of mind. Over the past twenty years he has frequently spoken of the mystical and political aspects of Christian faith, thereby transposing into his own idiom two central themes of Dominican spiritual life — *contemplatio* ('contemplation'/mysticism) and *actio* ('action'/ politics). Exactly what he means by mysticism and politics will need to be examined later.

It is not enough, however, to emphasize the traditional provenance of Schillebeeckx's thought as a way of illustrating the pre-eminence of his work. His intellectual merit is not explicable merely in terms of his masterly command of texts from bygone eras. By profession he is a theologian. He is neither a philosopher, nor a sociologist of religion, nor a historian. As a theologian his profession is to talk about God, or rather about what people mean when they profess faith in God. As a Christian theologian, he discourses about God by speaking of Jesus of Nazareth. Thus, the two poles of his thought are the question of God and the question of the ultimate identity of Jesus. He dwells on the second to illuminate the first. These poles or themes dominate the entirety of his publications. His publications are resolvedly theocentric, that is, focused on belief in God. Consequently, to state the obvious, he is recognizable as a theologian. His writings are also decidedly Christocentric, which is to say, they expound faith in God by constantly referring to the figure of Jesus of Nazareth who is commonly confessed as the Christ, or the Anointed One of God. Hence, Schillebeeckx is also describable as a *Christian* theologian. His works provide a conceptually sophisticated guide, based on attention to present-day experiences, for anyone posing the two cardinal questions of Christian theology, 'Who is God?', and 'Who is Jesus?', in the midst of the problems, convulsions, and conjunctures of our times. Again and again he returns to ponder these questions from different angles and in diverse contemporary settings.

CONTEMPORARY EXPERIENCE

Herein lies a second explanation for Schillebeeckx's significance as a Christian thinker. His thought analyses present-day experiences in addition to past texts and traditions. In his life-long quest to interpret Christian faith in God, he does not rely solely on texts from the past. Especially in his more recent studies he draws from an extensive body of literature that analyses contemporary human experiences philosophically, linguistically, anthropologically, politically, historically, sociologically, and psychologically. As a result, his significance as a Christian thinker also needs to be explained in terms of his ability to use contemporary ideas and understandings of human existence to shed light on what belief in God might mean for current circumstances. One British academic commented recently that 'most theologians are in fact critical historians who study and interpret texts from the past'.[7] Schillebeeckx's works are not based on past texts, but on analyses of human experiences, both past and present, as these are codified in writings, and undergone in traditions and communities.

ENCOUNTER, HUMANITY, AND NEGATIVITY

Hitherto, I have explained Schillebeeckx's position as an outstanding Christian thinker in terms of his command of Christian tradition, and his attention to contemporary human experiences. One further factor that illustrates his prominence as a Christian thinker also needs to be stressed, and that is his originality or imaginativeness. While he shares many ideas in common with other theologians, he has offered in an original and noteworthy way three major notions for consideration by twentieth-century inquirers into Christian faith. Otherwise put, one of his contributions to twentieth-century theology has been his attention to the notions of encounter, humanity, and negativity.

The idea of encounter is salient in his early work and is consonant with early twentieth-century existentialist philosophies that concentrated their reflections on the human person rather than on abstract concepts. For a generation of Europeans seared by world wars, Schillebeeckx's language describing a personal encounter with Jesus as a personal encounter with God fell on receptive ears (see CS). His language was perceived as a more engagingly personal manner of commenting on God and Jesus than a good deal of post-sixteenth-century Roman Catholic theology which frequently operated at high levels of abstraction without sustained attention to individual human experiences.

Schillebeeckx's notion of humanity functions in three significant ways. In relation to God, it operates so as to emphasize that a complete definition of humanity is only reached in God, so to speak. In other words, God's very being involves humanity. Whereas one might be inclined to separate sharply human and divine realities, for Schillebeeckx reality is one and selfsame, and that which is worldly and human is included in the divine. Rather than conceiving of God as a separate thing set over and against the universe, Schillebeeckx stands in a long Dominican tradition of imagining all things as being intelligible only *in* the reality of God.[8]

In a second setting, Schillebeeckx's theme of humanity also plays a determinative role and that setting is the field of Christology (discourse on Christ). Wherever it is postulated that in the figure of Jesus Christ there are two realities, one divine and the other human, Schillebeeckx has originally and deftly clarified in the latter part of the twentieth century that the reality and identity of Jesus cannot be dualistically dichotomized. For Schillebeeckx, especially in his writings of the past thirty years, the reality of Jesus was and is unitary. Jesus' indivisible reality can be spoken about from two fundamentally different though related perspectives. From a historical, anthropological stance he can be described and interpreted in terms of his humanity. But from a perspective of religious faith he can be spoken of in terms of his relation to God—his divinity. Yet whatever is meant by his divinity is located in his humanity—not outside it, parallel to it, above or below it. A good deal of classical Christology (of the past fifteen hundred years) has maintained that Jesus is able to be proclaimed as saviour because his humanity is fused (ontologically linked), so to speak, with the reality of God the Father. Schillebeeckx has moved in the direction of asserting that the salvific significance of Jesus is best comprehended in view of his humanity itself which may be regarded as a personal manifestation in human history of what God is like.

A third significant way in which the notion of humanity functions in Schillebeeckx's theology is to specify the distinctiveness of Christianity. According to Schillebeeckx, Christianity 'humanizes' religion in the sense that it is inherently concerned with human integrity (GAU, p. 157). In contradistinction to religions that posit a sharp cleavage between an utterly distant and transcendent God and a humanity with which God does not directly associate, Schillebeeckx maintains that for a Christian God is involved with all that is human. He often quotes St Irenaeus (*c*. 115–190) for whom it is not necessary to negate the honour of humanity in order to affirm the honour of God. With Irenaeus in mind Schillebeeckx goes on to assert that to seek a more enhanced humanity in the midst of suffering and inhumanity is to seek God. With reference to the notion of humanity, Schillebeeckx's originality resides in the way he has brought the notion to the centre of his discussions about

God, Christ, and Christianity. While many theologians would define the distinctiveness of Christianity in terms of the uniqueness of its idea of God as Trinity, Schillebeeckx elaborates on Christianity's unique identity in categories of the humanity of God and of Jesus.

As for the concept of negativity, it has undergirded Schillebeeckx's works especially since the mid-1960s. At that time he once spoke of having 'an almost feverish sense of urgency' to find a way of reinterpreting Christian faith so as to help believers who were confused about faith or leaving churches in the face of secularization and a superabundance of competing views of human existence (GFM, p. 169). Whereas, to speak in the broadest of terms, before the twentieth century Christian understandings of the cosmos and human nature were recognized in Europe's and its colonies' social organizations, in more recent times, Christianity is normally no longer the explicit intellectual and cultural foundation of Western governments. Today, Christian views concerning the cosmos and human nature compete in a market-place with Marxist, atheistic, Buddhist, Muslim, and all manner of other movements. Confronted by a pervasive profusion of philosophical world-views, Schillebeeckx searched for a human experience that could serve as a universally accessible and intelligible basis for explaining the meaning of Christian faith to audiences that might not share traditional Christian concepts and assumptions. The experience he came upon was one of negativity or suffering. In his early works he relied on a particular philosophical current for speaking about God and Jesus. But in his later works a singular philosophy is no longer so recognizable as a privileged medium for clarifying faith. Instead, that medium becomes a negative experience of suffering.

We come closer now to locating the nucleus of Schillebeeckx's thought. Obviously, Christian faith has a specific history. It was initially lived and proclaimed in Eastern Mediterranean territories two thousand years ago. It was never a disembodied belief in an abstract idea, because it was centred on *someone*—a Galilean Jew called Jesus who was heralded as an unparalleled human disclosure of God. There is no side-stepping the situation that Christians of antiquity maintained that Jesus was the centre of human history and of decisive importance for all people. Their faith was verbalized in the languages and concepts of ancient epochs. Yet the Christian gospel is no longer preached in the Mediterranean cities as they existed in Jesus' time. Nor is it studied any more in the bygone, now ruined cloisters of mediaeval Europe. Currently, it is lived in an altogether different kind of world. It is expressed in a multinational, polycentric, pluricultural gathering of countries competing for resources on a planet choking in its own pollution. It is professed in the face of twentieth-century disbelief and religious indifference. It is questioned in cultures transformed by industry, electricity, satellites, and computers; on a planet where people can travel at the speed of sound and communicate at the speed of light; in nations traumatized by the recent history of world wars; and among peoples perplexed, challenged and menaced by the daunting powers of technology and science. For the moment, Christian faith is not announced in a world that equates either culture with Europe or religious belief with Christianity.

Because of a distance in time between ancient and modern periods, and on account of the striking disparity between age-old and new-born human experiences, a pressing question arises for a Christian theologian: How should faith be lived and formulated afresh and with a view to future generations? By a literal repetition of time-worn creeds and dogmas? By a radical renovation of theological language? By a total eclipse of venerable traditions of yesteryear? In other words, what ensures that contemporary expressions of Christian faith have anything to do with original faith-proclamations?

To follow the development of Schillebeeckx's thought is to chart an evolution in the way he responds to these questions. In the late twentieth century, Christian churches have been unsettled by a perceived disjunction between contemporary experiences and thought-patterns, and classical ecclesiastical language and structures. How frequently does one hear it said that Christian churches are in the midst of a dispiriting crisis? A fundamental and underlying problem at the heart of whatever ecclesiastical anxiety there is in our times stems in part from the fact that particular ecclesiastical customs and forms of speech are moulded by specific concepts of previous times; concepts concerning God, human existence, and the world. Contemporary churches are organized in the main according to ideas stemming from the past. Considerable disruption has unnerved churches lately because new human experiences and concepts hitherto unknown to humankind have not been incorporated adequately into present structures and language as the churches face the future. Forms and structures from the past remain in place while the experiences that gave rise to them are no longer in sight, and while new ideas about humanity, the world, and God have not yet found expression in new forms and structures.

Schillebeeckx's professional career as a theologian has been much exercised by the problem of sifting peripheral and dispensable ideas and structures in Christian churches from the intrinsic underlying basis of Christianity. In other terms, he has been much exercised by the task of explaining the specificity of Christianity or of what guarantees that a particular way of living and proclaiming religious belief is actually *Christian*.

CREATION

During Schillebeeckx's long and evolving search for a suitable explanation of Christian identity, or of what has been called frequently the quest for the essence of Christianity,[9] he has persistently relied on a particular view of creation (as we shall see in Chapter 5). If one word designates the nucleus of his theological thought, then that word is 'creation'. Creation is the mainspring and master-concept of his theological corpus. And so, to appreciate the cohesiveness of his overall theological output it is necessary to grasp what he means by creation. For Schillebeeckx, the essence of Christianity includes a twofold belief in God as Creator, and in Christ as the condensation of all that is entailed in creation. Within such a view, neither dogma nor doctrine is the warranty of Christian faith's authenticity. The warranty does not lie in conceptual means for enunciating faith, but in the reality referred to by formulations of faith, namely, God.

Within Schillebeeckx's theological writings, therefore, all roads lead to creation. A Schillebeeckxian catechism would run something like this: Who is God? God is Creator and saviour of all. What is reality? Reality is a divine creation. Who is Jesus Christ? He is the condensation (see p. 94) or encapsulation of the reality of creation. What are human beings? They are creatures existing in a divine creation. What is the ecosphere? It is part of a divine creation.

Schillebeeckx's creation-based theological enterprise distinguishes his work from many forms of nineteenth and early twentieth-century Catholic theology. His particular reformulation of faith in creation sets him apart from a host of contemporary theologians. The way he understands creation explains why he speaks about God's relation with humankind in a manner totally different from, let us say, Catholic theologians such as Karl Rahner (1904–84), Bernard Lonergan (1904–84), Hans Urs von Balthasar (1905–88), and Hans Küng (b. 1928).

But that is not all. Schillebeeckx's views on creation have enabled him to avoid a major pitfall in contemporary philosophical discussions about God, that is, the idea that God can ever be known or discussed *solely* from the vantage point of an isolated, self-sufficient, human cognitional subject. Technically speaking, this pitfall may be tagged as epistemological (relating to a theory of knowledge) evidentialism, which is the view that God can be either proved or disproved, as it were, on the basis of evidences produced by a human rational subject. It is a breathtaking historical irony that modern atheism and many forms of post-Baroque Roman Catholic theology share exactly the same philosophical premise when it comes to discussing human knowledge of God. That premise turns on the conviction that God's existence may be known and proved merely and primarily on the basis of the cognitional powers of an individual human subject operating in abstraction from history and other human beings. Schillebeeckx's thought starts from, develops, and returns to the notion that reality is a divine creation. It is one vast digression from this notion. By definition, so he says, human beings are related to a Creator, and to all things, living and inanimate, in a divine creation. People know God because they live in God, as it were. In other words, a human being exists, by definition, in relation to God as an effect is related to a cause.

By relying on the theme of creation as the foundation of his theology, Schillebeeckx unveils himself as a resolutely traditional thinker. Creation was of utmost importance for St Thomas Aquinas (1225–74). As we shall see, though, Schillebeeckx departs substantially from Aquinas's way of interpreting it. Thomas's writings on creation flowed from a single idea: goodness is self-diffusive. Otherwise expressed, the goodness of God manifests and diffuses itself in creation. God and non-divine people are not set over and against each other, because humans are created in God's image. On this point, Schillebeeckx is in full agreement with Thomas and is inclined to describe human beings as the story of God.[10] For Schillebeeckx, humanity is the fundamental symbol or cypher of the divine. It is the diffusion of God—the Absolute Goodness—in this world. One of Schillebeeckx's favourite expressions for describing God is to say that God is a Pure Positivity.[11] All of which is to assert that there is no negativity or evil in God who is an Absolute Goodness.

SALVATION

Linked to the theme of creation in Schillebeeckx's writings is the motif of salvation. His recent publications draw attention to what he regards as a striking historical irony in the late twentieth century. He finds it ironical that the cultural forces such as science and technology that once presented themselves as the salvation of humanity in place of religion can now be seen as the very potencies which threaten humanity's continued existence. He has no quibble with either science or technology as such, but only with specious claims that such forces can liberate humankind from limitation and suffering (III, pp. 1–4). For Schillebeeckx, the ironical situation of the self-proclaimed deliverers of salvation turning out to be death-dealing threats to human well-being and salvation poses anew the whole question of salvation: Who or what saves human beings from everything that bedevils them? God, or human agents (see JWC, pp. 1–14)?

His answer is once again linked to the idea of creation, for ultimately, he proposes, it is the Creator God who saves. According to Schillebeeckx, creation is the first stage of a history of salvation in which God is given to human beings as their salvation.

So much for the very general and prefatory remarks I have been making regarding Schillebeeckx's theology. To tease out what I have been alluding to thus far, we may now embark on a more discerning exploration of his life and thought.

Notes

1   There is no complete bibliography of Schillebeeckx's writings, but for a listing of works published up to 1983 see Robert J. Schreiter, 'A bibliography of the writings of Edward Schillebeeckx from 1945 to 1983' in Robert J. Schreiter (ed.), *The Schillebeeckx Reader* (New York: Crossroad, 1984; Edinburgh: T. & T. Clark, 1986), pp. 297–321.

2 Consult Ad Willems, 'The endless case of Edward Schillebeeckx' in Hans Küng and Leonard Swidler (eds), *The Church in Anguish: Has the Vatican Betrayed Vatican II?* (San Francisco: Harper & Row, 1987), pp. 212–22; Ted Schoof (ed.), *The Schillebeeckx Case: Official Exchange of Letters and Documents in the Investigation of Fr. Edward Schillebeeckx by the Sacred Congregation for the Doctrine of the Faith, 1976–1980* (New York/Ramsey, NJ: Paulist Press, 1984); Peter Hebblethwaite, *The New Inquisition? The Case of Edward Schillebeeckx and Hans Küng* (San Francisco: Harper & Row, 1980); and Harvey Cox, *The Silencing of Leonardo Boff: The Vatican and the Future of World Christianity* (Oak Park, IL: Meyer-Stone, 1988), p. 4.
3 See 'Mariologie, gisteren vandaag morgen' in Edward Schillebeeckx and Catherine Halkes, *Maria gisteren vandaag morgen* (Baarn: H. Nelissen, 1992).
4 See Edward Schillebeeckx, 'God, the Living One', *New Blackfriars* 62:735 (1981), pp. 357–70 (p. 363).
5 Throughout the remainder of this book I shall normally use the abbreviations listed on p. xvi to refer to Schillebeeckx's major publications in both the body of my text and in the notes. His articles and lecture material will be documented in the notes.
6 Consult Harvey Cox, *Many Mansions: A Christian's Encounter with Other Faiths* (London: Collins, 1988), pp. 2–4.
7 Don Cupitt, *Radicals and the Future of the Church* (London: SCM, 1989), p. 104.
8 See Jürgen Moltmann, *History and the Triune God* (London: SCM, 1991), pp. 156–64.
9 See Stephen Sykes, *The Identity of Christianity: Theologians and the Essence of Christianity from Schleiermacher to Barth* (London: SPCK, 1984).
10 As in the book, III.
11 See the article cited in note 4 above, p. 368; and JWC, p. 62.

2

Schillebeeckx's life in context

Explaining Edward Schillebeeckx's distinction as a Christian thinker necessarily calls for attention to his biography. Rephrased somewhat, his theology is biographical. His publications cannot really be prised apart from his life's history. Although anecdotal material is rarely evident in his writings, every article and book he has written has been produced from, and responds to, a specific circumstance impinging on his life. If he is not responding to an event or experience in his publications, then he is addressing an individual or current of thought. In short, his texts have contexts. Familiarity with the latter assists comprehension of the former.

This chapter surveys the historical, intellectual, and cultural setting of his life and works because the distinguishing characteristics setting him apart as an outstanding Christian thinker vary according to different stages in his career. For example, he excelled in the earliest phases of his academic career at scrutinizing ancient and mediaeval texts and inquiring into their historical background. In the mid-1960s his writings on the Church were given lustre through his direct involvement in the preparations for the Second Vatican Council in Rome (1962–65). In the late 1960s and early 1970s he threw himself fervidly into a study of scientific analyses of biblical texts and distinguished himself by becoming one of the first, if not the first, Roman Catholic dogmatic theologians of the twentieth century to incorporate extensively the results of scriptural studies that had developed over the past two centuries.[1] And in a more recent stage of his life, let us say, since the early 1970s, he has attempted to expound a Western theology of liberation in dialogue with Latin American and Asian forms of liberation theologies. In so doing he has distinguished himself by trying to elucidate the much-misunderstood and frequently neglected political dimension of Christian faith. More on that later.

WHAT'S IN A NAME?

Before describing the phases and signposts of Schillebeeckx's life, it might be helpful to explain his name. Even in Belgium the Flemish family name 'Schillebeeckx' is extremely uncommon. It has a history dating back to the Middle Ages and comes most notably from western Belgium around the city of Brugge (Bruges). While 'Schillebeeckx' is a Flemish word, 'Edward' is obviously English. The name 'Edward Schillebeeckx' also goes back to the Middle Ages when English influence in western Belgium was pronounced.

A rough English equivalent of the Dutch (including Flemish) pronunciation of 'Schillebeeckx' involves three syllables with a primary accent falling on the first: '*Skill*-a-Bakes'. The first syllable is rather more guttural than the English 'skill'. The second resembles the vowel at the end of the word 'Chin*a*'. The third has a long, open 'a' (as in 'day').

The meaning of the word is another matter and open to conjecture. As a family name it very probably designates 'those who come from the place where the stream separates'. The modern Dutch word for a small river or stream is *beek*. The Old Dutch term is *beeck,* which, in its genitive form, becomes *beeckx*: 'from the place of the stream'. The Swedish verb for 'separate' is *skilja*. The root *skil* is reflected in the Dutch term for 'difference', *verschil*, and in the verb *scheiden*, 'to separate'. Hence, by marrying words for separation and stream, we arrive at *Schillebeeckx*: 'the fork of a little river'. But more specifically, the word 'Schillebeeckx' may refer to the bar of earth that separates a single stream into forked streams.

So much for the name. For the purposes of an overview, Schillebeeckx's life and career may be divided into five major stages.

1. THE EARLY YEARS IN BELGIUM

Edward Cornelis Florentius Alfons Schillebeeckx was born in the Kingdom of Belgium on 12 November 1914. He remained in north-western and central Belgium during the first thirty-two years of his life and witnessed there the after-effects of two world wars.

Belgium is one of the smaller nations in Europe. It shares its borders with the Netherlands, Germany, Luxembourg and France. The area now known as Belgium was originally inhabited by Celtic tribes in the first century BCE. During the fourth century CE, Germanic tribes settled in the northern part of the territory. Modern-day Belgium is divided into nine provinces that form two principal linguistic groups. The linguistic divisions presently obtaining ultimately stem from the different tribes that originally occupied the region. Today, Belgians are for the most part recognizable as either Flemings or Walloons. The Flemings, the majority of the population, inhabit the northern provinces of the country. They speak Flemish—a variant of Dutch—and trace their origins to the Germanic clans that originally took root in their region. The French-speaking Walloons live in southern Belgium. A German dialect is spoken in corners of eastern Belgium.

Schillebeeckx is a Fleming. He was born in Antwerp (Flemish: Antwerpen; French: Anvers), the capital of the province of the same name, in a geographical region known as Flanders. While Flanders was once a dukedom confined to the north-west corner of Belgium, at present it includes the entire northern belt of the country. The city of Antwerp, situated on an estuary that flows into the North Sea, is a major centre of Flemish culture and one of Europe's most important seaports.

Neither of Schillebeeckx's parents came from Antwerp. He was born there in emergency circumstances shortly after the outbreak of World War I. On 4 August 1914, roughly three months before his birth, Belgium was invaded by a German army. German occupation continued until 11 November 1918. His parents, Constant J. M. Schillebeeckx (1882–1978) and Johanna Petronella Calis (1888–1974), were from Geel in north-central Belgium. For Belgians, Geel is an extremely well-known city, largely on account of its highly original manner of treating people with psychiatric illnesses. Almost every family in the city's environs was required to accept a patient from the city's psychiatric clinic and to integrate the patient into family life.

Schillebeeckx's parents established their home in Kortenberg, a small town that lies midway between Brussels and Louvain (Flemish: Leuven). Constant Schillebeeckx worked as a government accountant. When the Germans invaded, he and Johanna were visiting relatives in the region of Valkenswaard, a Dutch town that lies to the south of the city of Eindhoven and close to the border between the Netherlands and Belgium. The district of Valkenswaard is a heath frequently visited by Belgian holiday-makers. Because of the invasion, Johanna and Constant were unable to return directly to Kortenberg. They made a detour to Antwerp and waited there for three weeks until Edward was born. After his birth, they returned to Kortenberg where he spent his infancy. He may be described, then, as a Belgian, a Fleming, and by his own account, a 'Kortenberger' or 'Son of Kortenberg'.[2]

The fact that Schillebeeckx is Flemish bears emphasizing since he is occasionally and misleadingly categorized as Dutch. Throughout its history Belgium has been governed by different foreign powers: first by the Romans, then by the Merovingians and Carolingians. In the early sixteenth century it came under the Spanish-Catholic rule of the Habsburgs. At that time, Belgium, together with the Netherlands, formed what was previously known as the Low Countries. In 1609, however, the northern regions of the Low Countries gained independence from Spain, thereby precipitating the separation that still obtains between southern, largely Catholic Belgium, and the northern, more Protestant Netherlands. Belgium became a sovereign nation only in 1830.

Throughout its more recent history Belgium has never really

known Protestantism at close quarters. Roughly nine out of ten Belgians are still baptized as Roman Catholics. When Schillebeeckx was a boy, it was entirely possible for a Flemish child to grow into adolescence without ever knowing a Protestant intimately. Schillebeeckx's family was Catholic and demonstratively religious. As a boy he frequently accompanied his parents to early morning mass in the parish church of Kortenberg. The experience of serving mass as an altar boy stimulated an interest in becoming a priest, a fascination that was later brought to realization.[3] His family included fourteen children, with five girls and nine boys. He was the sixth child to be born.

Edward completed his primary education in Kortenberg, but at the age of eleven he was sent to a Jesuit boarding school in Turnhout. The city of Turnhout is located in the province of Antwerp, to the northeast of the city of Antwerp, in the northernmost recesses of Belgium. The Jesuits directed two schools in Turnhout: one for boys destined to join the Jesuits' ranks, or who had already begun to study philosophy as Jesuits; the other for boys who envisaged different lifestyles. Schillebeeckx attended the latter institution, although one of his older brothers was educated in the former before leaving for India to work as a missionary.

Edward's school was a Flemish establishment. Somewhat surprisingly, however, classes were conducted in French. It was not until the 1930s that the national government permitted at least some Flemish to be used in Belgian schools and universities. In 1930, the country was divided by parliamentary fiat into the two linguistic zones. When Schillebeeckx was in his teens, the notion still prevailed in Flanders that Flemish was not a suitable language for educating the young.

When Edward first arrived at Turnhout he did not know French and was required to learn it for his studies in such subjects as history and mathematics. He also studied Latin and Greek. He remained at the school for eight years. In his mid-teens his desire to become a priest intensified. He initially thought of enlisting in the Jesuits and of embarking for India like his brother. And yet, he hesitated. He was unsettled by what he regarded as the overly regimental and affectively stifled life at Turnhout, a school renowned for its disciplinary strictness. Because of his doubts as to whether he should become a Jesuit he launched himself on a systematic course of reading. He pored over the biographies of religious luminaries such as Sts Benedict (c. 480–547), Francis of Assisi (1182–1226), Dominic (1170–1221) and Ignatius of Loyola (1491–1556). He also came across Humbert Clérissac's book L'Esprit de Saint Dominique, a treatise that accentuates the way the followers of Dominic try to divide their time between study and engagement with people. During his final years at Turnhout Schillebeeckx's decision to become a Dominican began to crystallize.

One of the skills he developed at the school was the ability to play the clarinet as a member of the school orchestra. When he was about eighteen, a Belgian Dominican, Constant van Gestel (1899–1978), visited Turnhout to preside as guest speaker over one of the school's festivals. Van Gestel was known throughout Flanders for his regular Sunday evening radio addresses. Young Edward was playing the clarinet during the festival at which Van Gestel spoke. This was most probably the first time Schillebeeckx ever saw a Dominican.[4]

2. DOMINICAN EDUCATION: GHENT AND LOUVAIN

At the age of twenty, Schillebeeckx entered the Dominican Order. The Dominicans were founded by St Dominic in the early thirteenth century. Their official name, the Order of Preachers (*Ordo Praedicatorum*), partly defines their identity in the sense that they were instituted fundamentally to be an organization of preachers. Since their beginnings, they have attempted to imbue their preaching with the fruits of assiduous study. Expressed very plainly, Dominican life is a balancing act. It strives to hold in a creative equilibrium two mutually complementary activities: intellectual, contemplative preparation for preaching; and the activity of preaching itself in the many forms it can assume.

It was precisely these activities which initially drew Schillebeeckx to the preaching friars. Fifty years after he joined them he explained that they appealed to him because of their bipolar preoccupation with people and the study of religion (GNM, pp. 8–9). The Dominicans were theologically inviting for him because they traditionally advocated the priority of God's grace. In other words, they recognized that only God is absolute and that no religion, philosophy or theology can ever circumscribe the plenitude of God.

Significantly, Clérissac's book describes Dominican life in terms of three essential features that are, in turn, communal (coenobitic), academic, and apostolic.[5] Since the day Schillebeeckx became a Dominican, these features have remained permanent elements in his life: since 1934 he has always lived in a Dominican community (the coenobitic dimension); his primary profession has been to teach and write theology (the academic factor); and his theology has always sought to elucidate faith's meaning for others (the apostolic, pastoral factor).

Schillebeeckx's first years with the Dominicans were spent in Ghent, in north-western Belgium. Along with Antwerp, Ghent is a flourishing centre of Flemish culture. Formerly, it was the seat of the Counts of Flanders. A university was established there in 1816.

As a young Dominican Schillebeeckx was required to follow a long programme of initiation into the Order. He began his exercises as a novice in September 1934. For the next year he studied Dominican history and legislation, as well as mystical literature. At that time it was the custom of the Dominicans to give newcomers a new name. Schillebeeckx was called Henricus after the German Dominican mystic Henricus Suso (*c.* 1295–1366). This explains why most of his publications before the late 1950s were signed as 'H. Schillebeeckx'. At the end of his training as a novice, on 21

September 1935, he vowed obedience to the Master of the Dominican Order. He then set about studying philosophy.

When Schillebeeckx joined the Order it prescribed an initial seven-year course of studies for its initiates. The first three were called the *philosophicum* since they were devoted entirely to philosophy. The *philosophicum* was followed by the *theologicum*: four years of theology.

Thus far we have touched on the Belgian and Dominican contexts of Schillebeeckx's early life. To appreciate the kind of studies he undertook as a young Dominican, it is also enlightening to consider the broader context of studies within the Roman Catholic Church. 1914 was not only a time of war in European societies. It was also a period of considerable intellectual conflict in the microcosm of the European provinces of the Catholic Church. In June 1914, Pope Pius X (1903-14) directed that Catholic students of theology were to remain faithful to the teachings of Thomas Aquinas.[6] The following month, the Vatican's Sacred Congregation for Studies issued a list of twenty-four theses designed as a summary of St Thomas's teachings. All Catholic theologians were required to accept the propositions elaborated in the list. As a guide for theologians, however, the text was highly unsatisfactory not because it promoted Thomas's works, but because it abstracted his thought from history, transformed it into a shopping-list of philosophical dicta, and made no mention whatsoever of the New Testament. The list became a formidable instrument of power to prescribe a uniformity of method and content among Catholic theologians. It effectively sought to ensure that only one linguistic form—a high mediaeval one—could be used in theology.

Pius X's injunctions continued the efforts of Leo XIII (1878-1903) in the late nineteenth century to promote Aquinas as the exemplar of Catholic theology. In the intellectual and cultural turmoil unfolding in Europe after the French Revolution, the Catholic Church attempted to face the challenges of new political systems and ideas by renewing its institutions of learning with an accent on the work of Aquinas.

Before the Second Vatican Council, every twentieth-century Catholic theologian was educated according to the mind and method of Thomas Aquinas. Schillebeeckx was no exception. His *philosophicum* in Ghent included a detailed examination of the philosophical bases of Aquinas's philosophy. His *theologicum* involved a systematic reading of Aquinas's theology with the help of commentaries on Aquinas.

While the general pattern of Dominican and Catholic studies in the first half of the twentieth century was fixed on Aquinas, the *philosophicum* undertaken in Ghent was distinctive on two accounts: first, it paid great attention to the problem of God, or rather the problem of human reflection about God (GNM, p. 9); and second, it included courses given by the Flemish philosopher Dominic De Petter (1905-71). De Petter introduced his students to modern and contemporary philosophical literature as a complement to the ideas of Aquinas. In this he was quite exceptional. When Schillebeeckx was a student in Ghent, Catholic candidates for the ordained priesthood were forbidden to read philosophers such as René Descartes (1596–1650), Immanuel Kant (1724–1804), Baruch Spinoza (1632–77), or, to take a more recent example, Miguel de Unamuno y Jugo (1864–1936).

De Petter was a towering intellectual influence during Schillebeeckx's early life, and it was thanks to him that Schillebeeckx began to read philosophers such as Kant, Georg Wilhelm Friedrich Hegel (1770–1831), Edmund Husserl (1859–1938), and Maurice Merleau-Ponty (1908–61). Just one illustration of the importance of these philosophers for Schillebeeckx's later work concerns the figure of Husserl. We shall see later that Schillebeeckx's theological interpretation of Jesus' resurrection is guided by one of Husserl's primary philosophical axioms, namely, the principle of the intentionality of consciousness.

De Petter became a Dominican in Ghent in 1923 and went on to study philosophy and theology in Louvain. He returned to Ghent in 1931 where he eventually met Schillebeeckx during 1934. De Petter was responsible for teaching anthropology and metaphysics to Dominican students, and for accompanying their spiritual development (as Master of Students or *magister fratrum studentium*). As a philosopher he reinterpreted Aquinas's work with the aid of modern theories of knowledge, psychology, and sociology. He was particularly interested in phenomenology, a twentieth-century philosophy that analyses human experience and structures of consciousness.[7]

During the third year of his philosophical course, that is, between 1937 and 1938, Schillebeeckx began a research project under De Petter's direction. The goal of the project was to discover whether human reason is basically conceptual, or whether it includes non-conceptual elements (GNM, p. 13). While this might appear a rather sapless and inconsequential topic for a young friar, the philosophical problem involved has taxed Schillebeeckx's thought ever since. If the task of a theologian is to clarify how a transcendent God, that is, a God who is unconstrained by finiteness, is known by human beings in their finite history, then the theologian must be able to specify the aspect of finitude or finiteness in which contact with God can be made: Is it speculation? Conceptuality? Intuition? Emotion? Love? Music? Experience? Nature? Sport? Or any kind of action? As a young student Schillebeeckx concurred with De Petter's philosophy by concluding that human reason involves conceptual and non-conceptual components. Human contact with God is achieved in virtue of both components, but primarily through the non-conceptual factor. This conclusion stood in counterpoint to a good deal of conceptualistic theology of the time, that is to say, against a theology that presented itself as an ahistorical system of concepts.

As I have observed, Catholic theology in the late nineteenth and early twentieth century sought an intellectual countermeasure to what it perceived as the insidious cultural after-effects in the wake of the French Revolution. Its countermovement was unilaterally to impose Neo-Scholasticism (a modern revision of a mediaeval theology) in all Catholic educational institutions. While Schillebeeckx's theology betrays a clear debt to Aquinas and mediaeval thought, his work has never been Neo-Scholastic, largely because of the influence of De Petter. For it was De Petter who encouraged young Edward to balance attention to Aquinas with studies of modern philosophers and, in particular, of Merleau-Ponty.

Schillebeeckx finished his initial studies in philosophy in 1938 and immediately began military service in Léopoldsburg, to the south-east of Turnhout. The service was short-lived and rather more academic than military. In any event, it ended before the outbreak of World War II. Through the ministrations of an army chaplain, Schillebeeckx was granted long periods of time to study philosophy, psychology, and sociology. It is also worth noting that he read Karl Rahner's newly published study in philosophical theology called *Geist in Welt* (1939; the second, expanded edition of 1957 was translated into English as *Spirit in the World*, 1968). Later in his career Schillebeeckx enunciated his own pivotal philosophical principles in contradistinction to Rahner's interpretation of St Thomas in *Spirit in the World*.

After their studies in Ghent, Dominican students were sent to Louvain to begin their *theologicum* in a major centre of Dominican studies called a *studium generale* ('general house of studies'). De Petter moved to Louvain in 1939 to direct the programme of studies in the *studium*. After his brief stint with the army, Schillebeeckx moved to Louvain for his primary theological studies. Louvain is situated in the centre of northern Belgium in the province of Brabant. It is the site of an old Catholic university that was established in 1432.

When Schillebeeckx went to Louvain he studied in the Dominican house and not in the university. He became extremely dissatisfied with theological studies, largely because of the method used in the *studium*. The *studium* course consisted virtually of nothing else apart from a systematic reading of a mediaeval text — Aquinas's *Summa Theologiae* — elucidated with the aid of Baroque commentaries on Aquinas. Once again, the problem was not so much Aquinas's thought, which deeply influenced Schillebeeckx, but the identification of theology with the exposition of concepts that are not related to their historical context and to contemporary human experiences. During an interview given much later in life, Schillebeeckx described his initial theological studies as perfectly fruitless and useless (*vaines et inutiles*).[8]

De Petter was displeased with Schillebeeckx's attitude to theology and suggested he study the writings of the once renowned German theologian Karl Adam (1878–1966). Adam was a professor of theology at Tübingen, in Swabian Germany. He was widely read in Catholic circles before World War II, but after then he was almost forgotten on account of his support for the Nazis. He appealed to Schillebeeckx because he used contemporary biblical research and avoided mediaeval philosophical terms in his books. We have previously noted Schillebeeckx's interest in the task of specifying Christianity's identity. Karl Adam was greatly pre-occupied by exactly the same task. Apart from reading Adam, Schillebeeckx assuaged his displeasure with theology by continuing a private course of philosophical reading. He was eventually ordained to the priesthood on 10 August 1941. He continued to live and study in Louvain during the final years of World War II.

3. THE SOJOURN IN FRANCE: 1946–47

Schillebeeckx's life took a significant turn in 1946 when he went to live in France for postgraduate studies in theology and philosophy. Even though his stay there was a brief academic intermezzo, ending in 1947, it was a period of intense intellectual fermentation resulting in his conversion, so to speak, to theology.

While in France he pursued his studies in two places. From Saturday to Monday of each week he lived in a Dominican house of studies located at Etiolles near Paris. The house, called Le Saulchoir (from the French *saule*, meaning 'willow tree'), was at that time one of the more eminent theological schools in the Dominican Order. It is now defunct, but in 1950 it was responsible for the education of about a hundred students. Several of its professors advised bishops during the Second Vatican Council.[9]

The first Dominican theological school to bear the name L'Ecole du Saulchoir (The School of the Saulchoir) was established in 1904 at Kain in south-west Belgium. Its founders were French Dominicans who had been expelled from their country by anticlerical legislation. Its faculty and students eventually moved to Etiolles in the late 1930s. Like any other Catholic school of theology in the early twentieth century, Le Saulchoir d'Etiolles advocated a preference for St Thomas's theology. Unlike most other schools, however, its curriculum included an examination of the theological history of the eleventh, twelfth and thirteenth centuries, thereby elaborating the broad historical context of Aquinas's work. The curriculum was intended to base theological studies firmly and squarely on an analysis of primary historical sources, and not on secondary ones like the manuals (summary digests) which were popular in Catholic faculties during the first half of this century.

Schillebeeckx followed theological courses in Le Saulchoir d'Etiolles on Mondays, but from Tuesday to Friday he attended classes for advanced students in three Parisian state institutes of higher learning: the Université de la Sorbonne; the Ecole des Hautes Etudes (School of Higher Studies); and the Collège de France. In Paris he met Merleau-Ponty and Albert Camus (1913–60). At the Sorbonne and the Collège de France, he was interested mainly in philosophy. He studied phenomenological philosophy and the history of philosophy under teachers such as Jean Wahl (1888–1974) and Louis Lavelle (1883–1951). At the Ecole des Hautes Etudes he studied fourteenth- and fifteenth-century theology, as well as methods for analysing ancient texts.

Of all the teachers he encountered in Paris, none was more significant for his subsequent theological evolution than the Dominican friar Marie-Dominique Chenu (1895–1990). Indeed it was largely because of Chenu's approach to theology that Schillebeeckx became more inclined to develop his interests in the subject.

Chenu was a historian of the Middle Ages. He had been in charge of studies at Le Saulchoir d'Etiolles from 1920 until 1942, when he was dismissed from his post by the Master of the Dominican Order. In 1937, Chenu published a small study outlining an approach for renewing theological studies. The book, *Une Ecole de Théologie: Le Saulchoir* ('A School of Theology: The Saulchoir')[10] was condemned in 1942 by the Holy Office, a former department of the Vatican charged, among other things, with arbitrating doctrinal disputes in the Catholic Church.

In his book, Chenu underscored the importance of history for theology. Interestingly, he argued that speculative theories occupy a secondary place in theology, secondary, that is, to the realities referred to in formulas of faith. For our purposes this is an interesting position because it reflects the same standpoint as De Petter. Through Chenu and De Petter, therefore, Schillebeeckx was stimulated to relativize theology conceived as a conceptual system, and to place theological reflection in a historical (Chenu) and human-experiential context (De Petter).

After his displacement at Etiolles, Chenu went to live with Dominicans in Paris. He was invited to teach at the Sorbonne in one of its institutes and it was there that Schillebeeckx met him and followed his courses.[11]

Schillebeeckx was immensely impressed by Chenu's little book *Une Ecole de Théologie*. Yet there is much more to the significance of Chenu for Schillebeeckx than the former's interest in history. Chenu combined his academic endeavours with a direct engagement with French social problems. He encouraged groups of priests to undertake the same kind of (manual) work as French labourers. The theological idea behind this French worker-priest movement was called *présence au monde* ('presence to the world'), a term borrowed from the Dominican Henri Dominique Lacordaire (1802–61) and propagated by Chenu. The idea assumed that a priest's presence among (non-religious) workers could stimulate them to pose the religious question, that is, would make them wonder what motivates people who are involved with religion and, ultimately, would make them inquire about God.[12]

Schillebeeckx found a living realization of the Dominican ideal he had read about as a schoolboy exemplified in Chenu and his way of balancing studies and social-political engagement. With Chenu, Schillebeeckx finally discovered an appealing way of theologizing that was based on an attention to contemporary experiences and problems on the one hand, and a tradition of ecclesiastical reflection on the other. Schillebeeckx decided to prepare his doctoral dissertation under Chenu's direction and chose the relation between nature and supernature as a topic. It will be recalled that I mentioned in the last chapter that Schillebeeckx's thought grapples with an ever-present, overriding problem: the interplay between universality and particularity. The topic he chose for his dissertation was a transposition into theological terms, nature and supernature, of the philosophical categories particularity and universality. In any case, the topic had to be changed for pragmatic reasons. In 1947, Schillebeeckx was required in Louvain, to teach theology in the Dominican House of Studies. One of the subjects he had to teach was the nature of sacraments (sacramentology) and so for his dissertation he decided to write in the field of sacramental theology. But in so doing he continued to focus his thought on the relation between that which is universal and that which is particular; for, expressed at its simplest, a sacrament is a particularity that seeks to express something of an unseen God (*Deus absconditus*) who may be spoken of abstractly as universality.

4. THE PROFESSORSHIP IN LOUVAIN: 1947–57

Upon the completion of his studies in France, Schillebeeckx returned to Louvain where, in 1947, he was appointed a professor of theology in the *studium generale*. In that post he was required to teach a cycle of five theological subjects to Dominican students. Five other activities consumed his energies during the ensuing decade. First, he succeeded De Petter in the post of Master of Students in the *studium*. This meant that he was responsible for the spiritual development of about sixty students. Second, he wrote his doctoral dissertation, the preparation for which he had begun in France. Third, he published articles. Fourth, he worked as a chaplain in the local prison, occasionally saying Mass there and visiting inmates. Finally, in 1956 he was appointed a professor in Louvain's Hoger Instituut voor Godsdienstwetenschappen (Higher Institute for Religious Studies).

Between 1947 and 1957 Schillebeeckx's primary responsibility was to prepare Dominican candidates for ordination to the priesthood. His teaching focused on dogmatic theology—the discipline devoted to elaborating ecclesiastical doctrines that have been officially and solemnly proclaimed as encapsulations of Christian faith. His cycle of courses covered five principal topics: theological propaedeutics (introductory studies); sacraments; the theology of creation; the theory of Jesus' ultimate identity and import (Christology); and eschatology, or the discourse concerning ultimate things (such as life-after-death, Heaven, Hell, and Purgatory). In each course his method was dogmatic, that is, it accepted dogmas as a methodological point of departure and proceeded to expound them with the aid of philosophy, historical research, and references to Scripture.

5. LIFE IN THE NETHERLANDS

In 1957 Schillebeeckx left Belgium once again, but this time to live in the Netherlands. He moved from Louvain to Nijmegen, which lies on the River Waal in the eastern plains of the Netherlands, close to the Dutch border with Germany. It is the oldest city in the Netherlands, having been established by the ancient Romans. Schillebeeckx has lived in Nijmegen for more than three decades. During that time his thought has evolved in many different ways according to the kinds of events by which he has been confronted in the Netherlands. Once again, for the purposes of an overview it is helpful to divide his life in the Netherlands into three stages: (a) 1957–66; (b) 1966–82; and (c) 1983 to the present.

(a) Nijmegen: 1957–66

Schillebeeckx went to Nijmegen to take up a position as Professor of dogmatic theology and the history of theology in the Catholic University of Nijmegen. He arrived there towards the end of 1957 and settled in the Dominican House of Studies called the Albertinum (after St Albert the Great, 1193–1280). The Albertinum has been his base ever since.

After having lived in Nijmegen for about twenty-five years, Schillebeeckx described the impressions he had when he first went there: he thought he had returned to the Middle Ages (GNM, p. 15)! Such an impression could easily surprise anyone who imagines that twentieth-century Dutch Catholicism is an avant-garde, free-wheeling affair. When Schillebeeckx first arrived in the Netherlands, he encountered a Catholic Church that had experienced four hundred years of living in a region dominated by Calvinism. Broadly speaking, modern-day Flemish Catholics have tended to define their identity as believers in the face of unbelief and post-Enlightenment humanism, whereas Dutch Catholics have viewed themselves in contradistinction to Protestantism.[13] Ironically, Dutch Catholicism in the first half of this century was a type of strict Catholic Calvinism. One could say, while not wishing to stereotype either Catholics or Calvinists, that to be acceptable in Dutch society, Catholics needed to be as organized and as strictly observant as Calvinists. Today, Catholics form a minority in Dutch society, whereas in Belgium they constitute an overwhelming majority.

The strictness of the Dutch Catholic Church in recent times was partly a strictness of separation stemming from the way bishops in the late nineteenth century attempted to reorganize their churches. A Catholic hierarchy was re-established in the Netherlands in 1853. Before then, the region was considered as a mission land that fell more directly under Roman ecclesiastical jurisdiction.[14] Understandably enough, the newly established hierarchy attempted to create a cohesiveness and unity among Dutch Catholics. The result of these attempts bore fruit in the first half of the twentieth century when the hierarchy succeeded in insulating Catholics from other Dutch groups through the maintenance of an independent system of organizations. The hierarchy created Catholic social clubs, schools, political groups, a university (Nijmegen), a broadcasting centre, trade unions, and associations for different professions.

The Dutch refer to the way their society was divided into parallel groups as *verzuiling*, or compartmentalization. A Catholic compartment or column existed alongside a Protestant one, and these two alongside the State. This kind of segregation was weakened during World War II, in which the Dutch suffered terribly. Nijmegen itself was drastically damaged by bombardments. In time of war, national welfare took precedence over sectional interests, and Protestants, Jews, and Catholics worked together against a common enemy. And yet, the compartmentalization began again after the war. The southern parts of the Netherlands were liberated earlier than others. Because many Catholics lived in the south they were able to rebuild their religious cohesiveness.[15]

So much for the general religious situation in which Schillebeeckx found himself when he moved to Nijmegen. When he taught in Louvain his life was academic and cloistral. Soon after he arrived in the Netherlands he became involved with a wider public, both in his capacity as a university professor, and through his collaboration with the Dutch bishops as they prepared for the Second Vatican Council.

The Catholic University of Nijmegen was established in 1923 at the behest of the Dutch bishops as part of their drive to shield Catholics from the influences of Protestantism and liberal humanism. Even as a Catholic institution, though, the university was and is partly funded by the State.

When Schillebeeckx moved to Nijmegen, he encountered a different academic setting in addition to a diverse religious context. At Louvain, he had taught almost exclusively within the Dominican *studium generale*. Moreover, his students included young friars in both the early and advanced stages of their theological education. At Nijmegen, however, he was not a professor in the Dominican House of Studies, but in the university's faculty of theology. Importantly, his first students in Nijmegen were all graduates in theology and mostly priests. From his first Dutch appointment in 1957, until his retirement from the university in 1982, his primary teaching responsibility in the Netherlands was to lecture to postgraduates. Unlike his situation in Belgium, however, eventually he was able to teach women in the Netherlands. In addition, the new academic situation in which he found himself when he first arrived in Nijmegen meant quite simply that he had more time at his disposal since he was no longer the spiritual mentor of a sizeable group of young Dominican men. He had more time not only to undertake research, but also to travel. He established a firsthand contact with the concerns of Dutch Christians by accepting invitations to speak in many different parts of the Netherlands. This contact proved to be decisive for changing his theological method. In Louvain his method of teaching had always begun by explaining a specific dogma and its history. In a second step, the method moved on to explore what the dogma might mean for contemporary believers. In the Netherlands, however, Schillebeeckx began more resolutely to reflect theologically by taking human experiences as a methodological point of departure.[16]

Throughout his twenty-five years of teaching in Nijmegen Schillebeeckx followed basically the same pattern of organizing his lectures. The university required him to deliver four lectures a week and to direct a seminar. On Monday mornings he delivered two lectures in dogmatic theology to students of the faculty who were enrolled to follow his subjects. On Wednesday mornings he gave a lecture that was accessible to all students of the faculty, and indeed, to all students of the university. On Wednesday afternoons he lectured on the history of theology. He eventually discontinued these classes arguing that the history of theology should be integrated into dogmatic theology itself.[17] The first course he presented for his own students was on Christian eschatology. For the classes on Wednesday mornings he lectured on the Eucharist.

Before 1966 Schillebeeckx's lectures focused on topics such as eschatology, sacraments, the theology of culture, original sin, nature and supernature, and secularization. In 1963 John A.T. Robinson (1919–83) published his book *Honest to God*, a work that greatly preoccupied Schillebeeckx in the mid-1960s.

In 1961, two important developments marked Schillebeeckx's life. First, he helped to launch a new theological journal in Nijmegen — *Tijdschrift voor Theologie* ('Journal for Theology'). He became its chief editor and determined its purpose: it was to be a vehicle for Dutch-speaking theologians to treat contemporary subjects with a technical, scientific theological approach. In the second place, he began to become increasingly involved in the preparations for Vatican II. The convocation of the Council had been announced in 1959. In 1961, the Dutch bishops acted to prepare Dutch Catholics for the Council by publishing a letter addressed to all Dutch believers. The letter is a remarkably noteworthy document in that it presaged many of the major conclusions that were eventually adopted by the Council itself, conclusions, for example, concerning the collegiality of bishops and liturgical renewal. At the end of the letter the bishops thanked Schillebeeckx for his involvement in the text's preparation.[18] During all of the Council's sessions Schillebeeckx remained in Rome as the personal theologian to the Dutch primate, Bernard Cardinal Alfrink. Until 1966, therefore, one may conclude that Schillebeeckx's life in Nijmegen was absorbed by university teaching and work associated with Vatican II. In 1965 he was a foundation member of the new international theological journal *Concilium* ('The Council').

(b) Nijmegen: 1966-82

The year 1966 is one to be retained and highlighted at all costs in a consideration of Schillebeeckx's intellectual history. During it he visited North America for the first time. In Nijmegen he began to teach hermeneutics, or the science of interpretation. The whole period of the late 1960s turned out to be extremely eventful for him. In 1966 the Dutch *New Catechism* was published. Schillebeeckx had collaborated in its preparation for four years before its appearance. From 8 November to 20 December 1967, he visited the United States for the second time and lectured in several universities and colleges. In 1968, the Vatican's Sacred Congregation for the Doctrine of the Faith made known that it was investigating his theology, largely on account of his views on revelation. In 1970 he lectured briefly in England at the universities of Oxford and Manchester. During 1971 he became the first theologian to occupy the chair in Erasmus studies at Harvard University in Cambridge, Massachusetts. In 1976 his theology was officially investigated once more, though the bone of contention had become Christology. Issues concerning ministry in the Church provoked a third investigation in 1981. All of which indicates that Schillebeeckx has been under suspicion in certain quarters since the 1960s. He has never been officially censured as a result of these investigations.

(c) Nijmegen: 1983 and afterwards

Schillebeeckx retired from the university on 1 September 1982 and delivered his retirement speech the following year. Since then he has continued to be actively involved in the Dutch Catholic Church and to publish his researches. He has also continued as an editor of the review *Concilium*.

During the 1980s Schillebeeckx received widespread acclaim for his theological and cultural achievements. In 1982, for example, he became the first theologian to receive the European Erasmus Prize (Europese Erasmusprijs), for his contribution to European culture. In 1983 the Dominican Order's General Chapter, its highest governing body, designated his work and theology as a model for Dominican students. In the same year he was created a Commander of the Order of the House of Orange (De Order van Orange Nassau), which is the foremost civil honour in the Netherlands. In 1989 he also received the literary prize of the Golden Quill (Gouden Ganzeveer).[19]

Of his many activities in the Netherlands during the 1980s and early 1990s, two in particular deserve to be singled out. The first is his involvement in what are called critical communities in Dutch Catholicism. Somewhat akin to the basic ecclesiastical communities of Latin America, Dutch Catholic critical communities are smallish groups that recognize the primacy of local churches. Expressed differently, they draw attention to the integrity of particular churches and do not regard them as standing in second place to some kind of abstractly conceived supra-national Church. In brief, critical communities effectively stress the teaching of Vatican II that wherever the Eucharist is celebrated the Church is present ('Ubi Eucharistia, ibi Ecclesia').[20] Since the late 1960s Schillebeeckx has sought by deliberate preference to assist basic, critical communities. His preference is clearly recorded in one of his more recent books wherein he declared that he had written it 'as nurture for the faith of those who are at work in the base communities, to those who suffer and work there' (III, p. xv).

The second noteworthy activity in more recent years has been his involvement with a Dutch group that came into existence when Pope John Paul II (1978–) visited the Netherlands in May 1985. The group is called Acht Mei Beweging ('Eighth of May Movement').[21] It gathers once a year and does not enjoy the patronage of Dutch Catholic bishops. The founders of the group maintained that, during the Pope's visit, voices dissenting from his own would not be allowed to be raised in his presence. And so the movement gathered for the first time on 8 May 1985, around the time of the Pope's visit. On that day more than ten thousand members of the group met at The Hague. Schillebeeckx addressed the gathering, told his hearers that they had the right to be there, and reminded them that believing Christians can take issue with their leaders precisely because of a concern for their Church. The following year he addressed the Eighth of May Movement again, this time at 's Hertogenbosch, and spoke about the political significance of the Christian gospel.[22]

On 12 November 1989, seventy-five years after Schillebeeckx was born, a foundation devoted to the promotion of his work was inaugurated in the University of Nijmegen.

CONCLUSION

Such, in stark summary, are the more significant features of Edward Schillebeeckx's continuing life history. The five stages of his life outlined above involve changes of location and new experiences. Nevertheless, the direction that Schillebeeckx's life has taken has been impelled by a single, abiding absorption. The same absorption that animated the first stage of his career as an academic theologian has spurred him on ever since. That absorption is the eagerness to specify Christianity's identity by elucidating what faith in God and Jesus might mean for those unsure, denunciatory, or sceptical of faith. Schillebeeckx's quest for the meaning of Christian faith is the main focus of this book. The instruments he uses to enunciate his quest are explained in the next chapter.

Notes

1 By 'dogmatic theologian' here, is simply meant one who undertakes a scholarly analysis of Christian faith as it is proclaimed officially and solemnly — dogmatically — by the Church.

2   See Michel Van der Plas, 'Een verering die vriendschap werd: Edward
    Schillebeeckx over zijn vader en het geloof der vaderen', *Elsevier* 44
    (1988), pp. 136–41 (p. 136). This article has useful biographical infor-
    mation pertaining to Schillebeeckx. For an English-language account
    of Schillebeeckx's life see John Bowden, *Edward Schillebeeckx:
    Portrait of a Theologian* (London: SCM, 1983).

3   See GNM, pp. 2–3. This book contains a good deal of Schillebeeckx's
    biographical data.

4   I have no documentary evidence for this assertion, but make it on
    the basis of a recorded interview I had with Schillebeeckx in Nijmegen
    in 1990.

5   See Humbert Clérissac, *L'Esprit de Saint Dominique: Conférences
    spirituelles sur l'Ordre de Saint-Dominique* (Toulouse: Saint-Maximin,
    1924); revised English trans. (London: Burns, Oates, 1937).

6   See Pope Pius X, 'Doctoris Angelici: De studio doctrinae S. Thomae
    in scholis catholicis promovendo', *Acta Apostolicae Sedis* VI (Vatican:
    Rome, 1914), pp. 336–41.

7   For information on De Petter's life and work, the most complete
    study to date is the first of three projected volumes by Johan van
    Wyngaarden, *D. M. De Petter o.p. (1905–1971): Een inleiding tot zijn
    leven en denken*, Deel I: *Een conjunctureel-historische situering*
    (unpublished *licentiaatsverhandeling*; Louvain: Katholieke Univer-
    siteit te Leuven, 1989).

8   Edward Schillebeeckx, 'La Théologie' in *Les Catholiques Hollandais*,
    in conversation with H. Hillenaar and H. Peters (Brugge and Utrecht:
    Desclée De Brouwer, 1969), p. 3. Henceforth: 'La Théologie'.

9   See Jacques Pohier, *God—In Fragments* (London: SCM, 1985/
    New York: Crossroad, 1986), p. 20.

10 Marie-Dominique Chenu, and others, *Une Ecole de Théologie: Le
    Saulchoir* (Paris: Les Editions du Cerf, 1985: originally 1937).

11 Schillebeeckx, 'La Théologie', p. 4.

12 On the worker-priest movement, and Chenu's involvement with it,
    consult François Leprieur, *Quand Rome Condamne: Dominicains
    et Prêtres-Ouvriers* (Paris: Du Cerf, 1989).

13 Thus, Patrick Vandermeersch, 'Twee manieren van Geloven: Een
    historische belichting van het Vlaamse en het Nederlandse
    katholicisme', *Kultuurleven* 56 (1989), pp. 32–9 (p. 37).

14 See John A. Coleman, *The Evolution of Dutch Catholicism, 1958–1974*
    (Berkeley, Los Angeles, and London: University of California, 1978),
    pp. 24–36.

15 Peter McCaffery, 'The transition from unitary to pluralist Catholicism
    in the Netherlands 1920–1970' in Ian Hamnett (ed.), *Religious
    Pluralism and Unbelief: Studies Critical and Comparative* (London
    and New York: Routledge, 1990), pp. 52–63 (pp. 52–5).

16 See Mark Schoof, 'Masters in Israel: VII. The later theology of Edward
    Schillebeeckx', *Clergy Review* 55:12 (1970), pp. 943–60 (p. 948).
    Schoof's later publications appear under the name Ted Schoof.

17 For a description of Schillebeeckx's responsibilities in Nijmegen see
    Ted Schoof's article (in two parts), 'E. Schillebeeckx: 25 years in
    Nijmegen', *Theology Digest* 37 (1990), pp. 313–32; and *Theology
    Digest* 38 (1991), pp. 31–44. See especially, in the first instalment,
    pp. 317–22.

18 'De bisschoppen van Nederland over het concilie', *Katholiek Archief*
    16 (21 April 1961), cols 369–384 (col. 384).

19 See Mark De Caluwe, 'Hollande: Hommage au P. E. Schillebeeckx',
    Informations Dominicaines Internationales (1990), pp. 23–4 (p. 24);
    and Edward Schillebeeckx, 'Theologie, cultuur, politiek', *Dominicaans
    leven* 46 (1990), pp. 7–11 (p. 7).

20 See Adrian Hastings, 'The key texts' in Adrian Hastings (ed.), *Modern Catholicism: Vatican II and After* (London: SPCK, 1991), pp. 56–67 (pp. 58–9).
21 Consult Erik Borgman, Bert van Dijk and Theo Salemink (eds), *De Vernieuwingen in Katholiek Nederland: Van Vaticanum II tot Acht Mei Beweging* (Amersfoort/Louvain: De Horstink, 1988).
22 See FSG, pp. 151–9, esp. p. 156; and p. 160.

3

Schillebeeckx's sources

There are at least two fundamental preliminary steps to be taken in an attempt to grasp the essential features of Edward Schillebeeckx's theology. The first, undertaken in the last chapter, is to consider the biographical context of his work. We have seen that his publications were not produced in a vacuum, but shaped by his personal history in north-western Europe. The second is to examine the ancillary intellectual disciplines or sources that he harnesses to elaborate his version of Christian theology. Taking the second step might appear an especially bewildering undertaking because Schillebeeckx relies on a wide variety of intellectual sources to clarify what Christian faith in God and Christ might mean.

My purpose in this chapter is to outline in the broadest of terms a selection of the main intellectual sources Schillebeeckx relies upon in his publications. Most of the sources are different forms of twentieth-century Western philosophy. Others are historical; while some are biblical. Just as Schillebeeckx's writings may be regarded as a compendium of twenty centuries of Christian theological reflection, they may also be described as a guidebook to the development of Continental European philosophical reflection in our own times.

SCHILLEBEECKX'S USE OF PHILOSOPHY

When Schillebeeckx finally became interested in theology as a result of his association with Chenu in the mid-1940s, he never lost his initial attraction to philosophy. On the contrary, his writings give philosophical reflection a prominent place in his theological endeavours to explicate the sense of Christian faith. While philosophy is given a prominent place, it is not awarded pride of place. It is important to note that religious faith is always prior to philosophy in Schillebeeckx's writings. In other words, he does not rely on philosophy to prove or demonstrate God's existence, or to argue that God can be known by human beings. He has recourse to philosophy to explain what he regards as the essential meaning of Christian faith in a manner that is readily intelligible to any interested inquirer. He does not contend that belief in God can be either justified or gainsaid on the basis of philosophical argumentation. He argues that a decision either to believe or not to believe in God is taken by an individual in a pre-rational stage of human experience, that is, in a stage before an individual has been able to reflect explicitly about the integrity or otherwise of faith. According to such a view, explicit philosophical argumentation merely expounds the intelligibility of the pre-rational opting either for or against the possibility of God's existence (III, p. 64). For Schillebeeckx, the ultimate concern of theology is the comprehensibility of God (GM, p. 39). The main intellectual passion of his career has been to develop a *philosophically meaningful* and *humanly relevant* account of the notion of God.[1]

As for the matter of human knowledge of God, whatever that might mean and involve, Schillebeeckx does not deploy philosophical arguments to prove that God can be contacted and known within human history. Instead, he employs theories concerning the nature of human knowledge to explain how Christian faith may be regarded as a legitimate form of knowledge. The question of what it means to profess that God can be known by human beings is central to Schillebeeckx's theological enterprise and will be examined later in a separate chapter.

While philosophers by profession are at liberty, and frequently do attempt, either to establish or discount God's existence on the basis of philosophical inquiry, Schillebeeckx enjoins the view that in this world God cannot, has never been, and never will be demonstrated discursively by human beings relying simply on their rational powers (see III, pp. 64 and 75). In taking this stance he is not advocating a philosophical scepticism. He is not primarily a philosopher, but a theologian. It is precisely as a theologian that he disavows assertions that evidence for God's existence or non-existence can be weighed conclusively through philosophy. His disavowal, therefore, is doxological (rendering praise): it is a form of praising God in the recognition that God could not possibly be circumscribed by the activities of human thinking and inquiry. For Schillebeeckx, a theologian must safeguard God's transcendence, that is, point out continually that God is not hidebound or adequately described by human concepts (III, pp. 4, 58, 74, and 99–101).

By the same token, however, Schillebeeckx does not imagine that Christian faith can exist in a kind of storm-free zone immune from the exigencies of rational argumentation. From the moment a believer talks about faith, it becomes incumbent on the believer to expound it in a way that would be intellectually comprehensible to believers and non-believers alike. The forbidding question at issue here is whether religious faith may be regarded as rational. While it is not rational in the same way as a purely logical exercise is, it is not without reason. In short, it is not irrational. Logical rationality may well prove that all cats have heads, but it cannot demonstrate the validity of Christian faith's claim that Jesus Christ is alive. By what means could it? Faith refers beyond logic and is not based exclusively on reason. Or, to paraphrase Shakespeare, there is more under the heavens than has been dreamt of by philosophers.

THREE PHILOSOPHICAL INTERESTS

So much for the way Schillebeeckx relies on philosophy in relation to faith and theology. Now for a word concerning his primary philosophical interests. From his earliest to his latest publications, there are three philosophical interests that consistently undergird his theological reflection. Tracing the development of these concerns greatly assists a comprehension of his theology. The first is ontological (relating to being) and metaphysical (concerning the nature of [intangible] reality): it concentrates on the intrinsic nature of being or reality. Its driving question is 'What, in the long view, is reality?' The second is epistemological, which is to say, it concerns the nature, limits, and scope of human knowledge. In particular, it poses the question as to whether and in what manner human beings could know God. The third is anthropological in that it seeks to explain what it means to be human.

These three interests — ontology and metaphysics, epistemology, and anthropology — are philosophical threads running through the length and breadth of Schillebeeckx's publications, even though one rarely finds him speaking explicitly of ontology or metaphysics in his more recent writings. There are two difficulties, however, in attempting to follow the development of his reflection on these threads. First, he is not given to long, explicitly philosophical discussion in his writings. More often than not, his analyses of philosophical terms are frustratingly sketchy. The philosophical expressions that are operative in his theology are often explained only tacitly. Try, for example, to find in his writings a clear and succinct explanation of his particular understanding of the notion of *praxis*. Praxis, it would seem, is a term first used in a technical philosophical sense by Aristotle. But in its subsequent history it has been invested with many different meanings. The term occurs with unremitting frequency in Schillebeeckx's writings of the past twenty-five years, but he does not spell out in any detail what he means by it. All of which is to stress that, in order adequately to comprehend his theology, it becomes a pressing requirement to ferret out and throw into sharper relief the philosophical postulates that are implicitly imbedded and referred to in his writings. In the second place, while there are philosophical positions that have remained permanent fixtures of his theological reflection, there are others which have appeared only in his more recent publications. In other words, his manner of using philosophy in theology is both consistent and inconsistent, continuous and discontinuous.

There is an obvious reason why Schillebeeckx is disinclined to expound philosophical problems at length in his works. In the long run, he is not at all immediately concerned to unravel philosophical enigmas once and for all. His impelling ambition is at once more modest and more pastoral. His works are driven by a concern to help people who find Christian faith either incredible, meaningless, or destructive.

In outlining the non-theological intellectual sources relied upon by Schillebeeckx in his publications, a subsidiary aim of this chapter is to explain a major philosophical change in his thought during the 1960s. His writings of that time are unrelievedly punctuated by three words: crisis, newness, and change. Because of a supposed crisis of faith that he perceived among North American and European believers, and in the light of experiences hitherto unknown to humankind, he changed the style of his philosophical argumentation while retaining philosophical postulates that underlaid his early writings.

This change is especially evident in his epistemological and anthropological propositions which are themselves founded upon a more basic ontological supposition (concerning a divine creation) which sustains his theology. Moreover, of the various kinds of philosophical interests traceable in his work, the epistemological is by far the most predominant and recurrent. He once commented that even though the question of the precise nature of human knowledge of God may appear academic, it is nonetheless 'a matter of "to be or not to be" for religion' (GM, p. 169, n. 11). This is so because religion, viewed as an interrelationship between God and human beings, becomes meaningless and devoid of content if it does not involve a positive knowledge about God. By displaying a primary interest in epistemology within his works, Schillebeeckx reflects a thoroughly modern philosophical preoccupation to determine what can be known indubitably by human beings. Even so, his works are intrigued not by epistemological questions as such, but by problems associated with religious epistemology. Stated differently, they discuss theories of knowledge in so far as these could be used to elucidate the nature of religious knowledge. For Schillebeeckx, a burning philosophical question for theology is this: Does a believer have a direct (cognitive) relationship with God or not? (see II, p. 809). Both his early and later writings reply that a believer does. They differ, though, in the patterns of arguments they deploy to elucidate the kind of cognitive relationship that is said to be involved.

The crucial issue of change in the philosophical presuppositions underlying Schillebeeckx's theology may be sketched as follows. First, there is the matter of ontology, and with regard to that, the issue of consistency in his reflection. Throughout his career, he has understood reality as a divine creation. All other philosophical postulates at work in his publications are based on this conviction. Within his writings it operates in two ways. In the first place, it is professed as a conviction of faith, but precisely as such, and in the second place, it functions simultaneously as a philosophical-ontological postulate. For Schillebeeckx, faith and philosophy are not concerned with two different dimensions of that which is real, but with one and the same reality.[2] Less change is discernible in his basic ontological position than in his epistemological and anthropological theories. Even so, his ontology did not remain unsettled by the crises that he observed in the mid- and late 1960s. After the mid-1960s, for instance, he became more convinced that reality is characterized by an illimitable pluralism: it is so complex that it cannot be described or understood by any single human, explicitly conceptual perspective. Moreover, reality is not static, but an open-ended and dynamic process. Consequently, rather than decrying a plurality of religions, or an abundance of different Christian churches, one may conclude that plurality is a principle or distinguishing feature of reality.[3]

With regard to epistemology, Schillebeeckx has always argued that perception is the basis of all human knowledge and that human beings can know God only as a result of God's manifestations in the world of creation. And yet, within his early writings he discusses religious knowledge, that is, human knowledge of God, in terms of an individual's inner life of grace. In his later works he speaks of religious knowledge in categories of social action and ethical praxis. Once again there is a detectable continuity and discontinuity in his style of philosophical argumentation.

In the third instance, we come to the anthropological foundation of Schillebeeckx's theology. As a young man he studied the works of the twentieth-century French existentialist philosopher Georges Gusdorf (b. 1912), and subscribed to the latter's opinion that a person is not a fixed, self-standing reality, but an ongoing history. Throughout Schillebeeckx's writings he has persistently characterized a human being as a 'situated freedom'. If God the Creator is an absolute freedom, unconstrained by any limitation whatsoever, then a human being is a particular situated freedom. In addition, a human being receives his or her freedom from God through the divine act of creation. In sum, a person is neither a pure nature nor an inert thing, but an evolving narrative or a free and active historical event. In the later 1970s, however, Schillebeeckx considerably amplified the anthropological aspects of his writings by underscoring the multiplex features of human existence.[4]

A point to be re-emphasized here is that all of Schillebeeckx's primary philosophical interests are linked to the notion of creation: a human being, as a created situated freedom, may know God through divine manifestations in the reality of creation. Ontology, epistemology, anthropology, and theology are thereby all intertwined in Schillebeeckx's publications and theological argumentation.

At this juncture, I would like once again to illustrate the extent to which Schillebeeckx's theology is rooted in a classical theological tradition. Thomas Aquinas taught that while human beings cannot know or define God's essence, they can at least make explicit affirmations about the divine because God is manifested in effects, that is, through creation (see Thomas's *Summa Theologiae*, I, q. 1, a. 7, ad 1). Transposed into other terms, the divine discloses itself in relation to human experiences of creatureliness (or contingency). Schillebeeckx's entire theological corpus is one vast digression from this fundamental point and an extended variation of Aquinas's theme. Throughout his theological career Schillebeeckx has attempted to specify the particular human experience from the vantage point of which it becomes possible to talk of the divine. In his early works that experience was said to be an ecclesiastical sacrament. More recently, it has been designated as, to use his own terms, a negative contrast experience. Of which more later (see pp. 127-9).

To make more sense of the non-theological sources employed by Schillebeeckx in his theology, and to understand better the causes and consequences of his philosophical turnabout in the 1960s, we may begin to outline his use of the sources by attending to the first half of his theological career. The time of decisive philosophical change in his reflection transpired around 1966. In a sense, one may speak of the early and later Schillebeeckx, or the pre- and post-mid-1960s Schillebeeckx, on the basis of new philosophical preoccupations and styles of argumentation that were etched into his mind around 1966.

THE INTELLECTUAL SOURCES OF SCHILLEBEECKX'S WORK

At the beginning of this chapter I noted that most of the sources Schillebeeckx relies upon to enunciate his theology are forms of twentieth-century Western, Continental European philosophy. However, apart from philosophy, he also depends most notably on historical, biblical, and sociological studies. When pondering the different sources referred to in his writings it is as well to recognize: (a) that his acquaintance with them might occasionally be cursory; and (b) that he might cull certain ideas from sources while entirely rejecting others. In his early work, for instance, he frequently discusses French existentialism without necessarily subscribing to every existentialist tenet.

In listing Schillebeeckx's more significant sources below, no attempt will be made to explain the nature and history of each one. Instead, for the rest of this chapter I shall concentrate only on the most basic and enduring influences on his theology. During the first two decades of his career as a theologian, that is, from roughly the mid-1940s to the mid-1960s, his theological researches were instructed by six major non-theological disciplines. The first four engaged his attention when he lived in Belgium and France. He came across the last two during his first ten years in the Netherlands. The sources are, in bare outline:

(a) The philosophy of Dominic De Petter;

(b) Historical studies (*ressourcement*) associated with the French

Dominicans of Le Saulchoir and French Jesuits of Lyon–Fourvière;

(c) Phenomenology, in both German and French expressions;

(d) French personalism and existentialism;

(e) Dutch humanism; and

(f) Sociological studies of secularization.

After Schillebeeckx's first visit to the United States in 1966, he began a frenetic search to reformulate the meaning of faith in God and Christ and the function of faith in secularized societies. Ever since the mid-1960s his theology has had recourse to a much more extensive variety of intellectual disciplines. Here is a list of the more significant among them:

(a) North American and Dutch philosophical pragmatism;

(b) Philosophical hermeneutics of the humanities;

(c) Historico-, form-, and redaction-critical biblical studies;

(d) Religious sociology;

(e) Practical-critical hermeneutics;

(f) Universal pragmatics;

(g) The Critical Theory of the Institute for Social Research (Frankfurt);

(h) Theoretical linguistics;

(i) Semiotics;

(j) Philosophies of language and linguistics, including phenomenological and logical linguistic analysis;

(k) Secular eschatology (Ernst Bloch);

(l) Psychology;

(m) Anthropology;

(n) Cultural historiography;

(o) Structuralism;

(p) Post-structuralism;

(q) Postmodernism; and finally,

(r) The philosophy of Emmanuel Lévinas.

Of the eighteen sources just listed, four are of utmost significance for an understanding of Schillebeeckx's later theology: hermeneutics, biblical studies, philosophies of language, and Critical Theory. Before attending to these and before explaining why Schillebeeckx turned to them in his theological explorations, we shall examine in more detail the nature and role of the non-theological instruments that serve his earlier work.

THE ANCILLARY DISCIPLINES OF SCHILLEBEECKX'S EARLY THEOLOGY

But first, I propose a rapid review of the anterior history of the sources Schillebeeckx eventually appropriated. During the seventeenth century, to speak in the most general of terms, there arose in Europe a marked philosophical preoccupation with the capacities of human reason and a suspicion that divine revelation has little or nothing to teach reason. This was the time of and for 'Enlightenment'.

In Immanuel Kant's pregnant observation, enlightenment is a person's liberation from self-induced bondage. And bondage or tutelage is a person's inability to understand without direction from another source (see Kant's germinal essay *Was ist Aufklärung?* ('What is Enlightenment?'), 1783). In short, to be enlightened is to use reason and not to cower unreflectively to authority, especially to an ecclesiastical authority whose authoritativeness is supposed to issue from a divine revelation. Whereas ancient and mediaeval philosophies had been greatly interested in metaphysics and cosmology, seventeenth- and eighteenth-century European philosophy was unmistakably absorbed by questions of reason and knowledge. Descartes and Kant were basically rationalist, ahistorical thinkers probing the question: 'How can I arrive at indubitable knowledge of something?'

For the sake of a summary, it could be said that before the eighteenth century, European thinkers shared a common view of existence, a view that was a fusion of ancient Greek metaphysics and biblical doctrines. Their reflections were focused on God, humanity, and the cosmos. With the Enlightenment, philosophy took a turn, so to speak, to the subject. That is, it concentrated more on the human subject as its primary theme. Nevertheless, the subject-centred, epistemologically dominated philosophies of the early Enlightenment began to cede ground in the eighteenth century to philosophies of science. The latter, in turn, held sway in the nineteenth century and colluded in the entrenchment of scientistic positivism, according to which natural sciences provide the sole access to genuine knowledge. For scientistic positivism, neither emotion, nor intuition, nor music, nor religion has a legitimate cognitive value. If a Greek metaphysical view of existence dominated pre-modern European circles, by the nineteenth century a variety of views competed for attention, views such as materialism, Marxism, idealism, Romanticism, humanism, historicism and positivism. We need not be waylaid here by trying to define each of these 'isms'. The point which needs to be brought home is that the hegemony of one philosophical perspective (among competing perspectives) in pre-modern times was significantly broken down in the twentieth century amidst a burgeoning of diverse and non-Western philosophical world-views. In bold strokes, then, we may sketch philosophical changes in Europe as a passage from metaphysics, to epistemology, to a plurality of philosophical perspectives, with scientistic positivism tending to predominate by the late nineteenth century.

The twentieth century witnessed both theological and philosophical reactions to rationalist and positivist thinking. It is these reactions that provided Schillebeeckx with sources for elaborating his early theology. Within Roman Catholicism, modernity was met with a strategy of counter-modernity (*adversus modernitatem*). Neo-Scholasticism was imposed in all Catholic institutes of higher education precisely as a countermeasure to the new intellectual currents that had evolved since the Enlightenment. As a countermeasure to democratic governments formed after the French and North American revolutions, Catholic leaders tended to regard the Bishop of Rome as a papal monarch. To this day, that bishop is called a sovereign. As we shall see, in Schillebeeckx's latest publications he has begun to raise the question as to whether the Church should more appropriately be regarded as a democracy instead of a community governed by an autocracy.

Be that as it may, at the beginning the twentieth century not all Catholics rebuffed modernity with its emphases on rationality, empirical science, human freedoms, and democracy. Within Catholic academic circles in the first half of this century there were a number of attempts to complement studies based on Aquinas's work with more modern disciplines. Two attempts in particular provided Schillebeeckx with sources for his early theology: Dominic De Petter's philosophy, on the one hand, and a historical approach to theology on the other. We will consider these before indicating the importance of phenomenology.

(a) De Petter's philosophy

Dominicus (Dominic) Maria De Petter was born in Louvain and entered the Dominican Order in 1923. During 1926, he received a doctorate in philosophy in Louvain with a dissertation on the French philosopher Louis Lavelle. Between 1926 and 1930 he studied theology and wrote a thesis on the epistemology of an older contemporary, Joseph Maréchal (1878–1944), who was a Belgian Jesuit based in Louvain. De Petter began to teach philosophy in Ghent during 1931, but moved back to Louvain in 1939 to direct the studies of Dominican students living there. In 1942, his Order relieved him of his responsibilities for the students. By then, his philosophy had encountered ominous opposition in Rome.

But why? Essentially because De Petter's philosophy interlocked Thomistic philosophy with phenomenology (to be explained shortly). In other words, De Petter was not content to teach philosophy merely according to ancient and mediaeval texts. He sought a renovation of Catholic thought through a critical appropriation of what he regarded as the sound gains of more modern philosophical traditions, and in particular, of phenomenology.

De Petter's overriding philosophical interests were metaphysics and epistemology. His research in those fields relied on two sources: Aquinas on the one hand, and the phenomenologies of Edmund Husserl and Maurice Merleau-Ponty on the other. In line with Aquinas, he was a metaphysical realist, which is to say, he believed that reality is not a product of human mental activities. He developed Aquinas's approach to knowledge in the context of phenomenology and insisted that human consciousness is not like a mirror that simply and passively reflects images of a reality external to consciousness: the perception of that which is real involves the thing or reality perceived (object), and an actively interpreting function of the perceiver's consciousness (subject).

This is not the place to explain De Petter's philosophy in minute detail. Suffice it to say that he was an important influence on Schillebeeckx because he sought to overcome philosophical conceptualism and dualism. He was convinced that all philosophy prior to Kant was metaphysically conceptualistic, that is, it reduced reality to the status of concepts, or, rephrased somewhat, it hypostasized concepts. He also surmised that modern philosophy was epistemologically dualistic, by which he meant that it divided too sharply objective (extra-mental) reality from subjective (perceiving) reality.

(b) Historical *ressourcement*

A second major source relied upon by Schillebeeckx's early work was associated with two French Catholic faculties: the Dominican school of Le Saulchoir, and the Jesuit school of Lyon–Fourvière. Both institutes were concerned to expound Christian doctrines by examining them against the backdrop of the doctrines' historical contexts. The Dominicans of Le Saulchoir advocated a theological method of inquiry with the catchword of *ressourcement*: 'back to the sources'. A good deal of Catholic theology in the first half of this century involved what Schillebeeckx has called 'playing with concepts' (GNM, p. 13). The professors of Le Saulchoir advocated a rejuvenation of Catholic theology by going back to a study of the historical circumstances that gave rise to particular doctrines. Hence, rather than attempting to understand Aquinas simply by reading his texts *in vacuo*, the *ressourcement* method examined his texts *in situ*, that is, with attention to the historical setting in which they were produced. While the Dominicans attended to historical sources of the eleventh, twelfth and thirteenth centuries, the Jesuits, whose enterprise was called the 'New Theology', concentrated to a greater extent on Patristic Christian writings.[5] Schillebeeckx studied the 'New Theology' in Louvain after he had returned from France where he had encountered the *ressourcement* programme of studies. It is important to note that neither the Dominicans nor the Jesuits sought to reinterpret Christian doctrines from the footing of a critical-historical analysis of biblical texts. What the proponents of *ressourcement* did do was to borrow methods worked out by biblical scholars in the nineteenth and early twentieth century. That which Biblicists called examining a biblical passage with regard to its setting-in-life (*Sitz im Leben*), the professors of Le Saulchoir labelled historical *ressourcement*. In any case, while Schillebeeckx's early writings are rich in historical information, they are nonetheless biblically pusillanimous. They quite frequently quote from the Bible, but methodologically their biblical quotations are subservient to, and relied upon to corroborate, officially proclaimed ecclesiastical doctrines.

(c) Phenomenology

We have already had occasion to observe that Schillebeeckx has studied many different philosophies during his career. The most significant one he explored during the 1940s and 1950s was phenomenology. This is hardly surprising since phenomenology was the most prominent form of philosophy in Europe from the 1930s to the 1960s.

Phenomenology involves an extremely amorphous and complex array of philosophical positions. Explained at its simplest, though, it is an anti-positivist philosophy developed in a significant way by Edmund Husserl around the turn of the twentieth century. Whereas positivism seeks to enunciate meaning and truth in terms of empirical experimentation, phenomenology is essentially an analysis of the nature and structures of consciousness. While the catchword of Le Saulchoir was *ad fontes*, or 'back to the sources', the watchword for phenomenology (from the word 'phenomena', meaning 'things') was 'back to the things themselves'. That is, phenomenology sought to examine the way things — whether they be multidimensional objects, ideas, or feelings — are apprehended by the structures of consciousness. In sum, phenomenology probed the issue of how the meaning and truth of reality is to be clarified; but unlike scientistic positivism, which regarded as truthful and meaningful only that which could be experimentally or materialistically corroborated, phenomenology spoke of meaning in terms of the (intentional) structures of consciousness.

In the early stages of his career Schillebeeckx countenanced the central insight of phenomenology, namely, the intentionality of consciousness. The principle of the intentionality of consciousness is a way of defining the definitive characteristics of conscious human experiences. According to the principle, consciousness by its very nature is always *consciousness-of* something. In other words, every act of thinking implies an object thought of; thinking is essentially thinking *about* something.

For the purposes of understanding Schillebeeckx's theology fewer notions are more worthy of attention than experience. In 1907, Pope Pius X debarred experience from being considered among Catholics as an appropriate source for theological reflection (see his encyclical letter *Pascendi Dominici Gregis*). Yet it is only inappropriate if experience is understood as a purely subjective and whimsically variable inner human state of emotion. Contrariwise, experience can be regarded as the only adequate basis for speaking of any reality whatsoever when it is more adequately comprehended as a form of consciousness involving an experien*cing* subject, and an objective reality experien*ced*. Husserl asserted that experience is a form of consciousness involving subjective and objective elements, and he defined experience as a consciousness of being with matters (things) themselves and of seizing upon them in a direct way.[6] For Husserl, experience is not a mere taking of something alien to consciousness into consciousness (as with naïvely realistic theories of knowledge). The upshot of adopting a phenomenological perspective is that the notions of pure objectivity and pure subjectivity are rendered nonsensical: there can no more be an object without a subject than there can be a subject without an object, just as there can no more be a known without a knower than there can be a knower without a known.[7] According to Husserl, subject and object are indivisible: an object only comes to be within experience in virtue of a subjective interpretation. Expressed differently, the principle of the intentionality of consciousness is fundamentally a matter of interpretation or the conferment of meaning: the experienced object comes to be within experience insofar as experiencing essentially involves the interpretation of certain material to permit a particular object to appear to consciousness within experience.

While Husserl employed phenomenological methods to analyse experience and human consciousness, Martin Heidegger (1889–1976) employed them to examine the question of Being in terms of an individual's day-to-day being-in-the-world. Jean-Paul Sartre (1905–80), on the other hand, analysed human freedom phenomenologically, while Maurice Merleau-Ponty advanced a phenomenological theory of bodiliness and human embodiment in the world. Paul Ricoeur (b. 1913) channelled his energies into a phenomenological analysis of signs, metaphors and symbols.

SCHILLEBEECKX'S MOMENTOUS PHILOSOPHICAL TURNABOUT

Much more could be said about early ancillary sources to Schillebeeckx's theology, but lack of space does not permit. Throughout his life-long quest to transmit and reinterpret faith, he retained central features of De Petter's philosophy, historical *ressourcement*, and phenomenology. His later writings, however, abound with discussions of new intellectual currents that are not examined in his earlier works. Before proceeding to elaborate on the more significant of those currents, it might be helpful at this stage to address the matter of a fundamental philosophical transformation, or turning point, that became evident in Schillebeeckx's writings in the mid-1960s. He came to the momentous realization that the ultimate meaning of human existence (universality) cannot be accounted for by a particular purely theoretical perspective.

For Schillebeeckx, theology must broach the universality/particularity problem mentioned in Chapter 1: it must attempt to explain how that which is absolute, true, and the totality of meaning (universality/God) can be perceived in that which is limited and particular (human history) (see GAU, p. 157). Both De Petter and the younger Schillebeeckx advocated a theory according to which an individual can know something of the totality of meaning, which can be named 'God'. In Schillebeeckx's later works, however, he denies that an individual can perceive something of the completeness of meaning. Instead, he argues that a totality of meaning can only be practically anticipated. This, then, is the most significant switch in Schillebeeckx's philosophical assumptions: a turnabout from asserting that the universality/particularity interrelationship can be explained in terms of a cognitive, theoretical apprehension of universality by a particularity, to asserting that whatever is universal can only be practically and partially anticipated in human actions.

This matter of universality and particularity and of a turn from a theoretical participation in, to a practical anticipation of, absolute meaning, may appear more than a little abstract, but it is a matter of unrivalled importance in Schillebeeckx's theology. This is so because he changed from theologizing from a largely abstract and theoretical perspective, to speaking about God in terms of human action. In other words, he changed from according a primacy to theories in his theological discussions to stressing that primacy ought to be accorded to human practices and actions which provoke reflection.

What caused Schillebeeckx to begin to accentuate the primacy of action and praxis in his theology? In a word, he became much more aware of the pre-eminence of the future in relation to the present and the past; of the historical nature of human existence; and of pervasive human suffering in contemporary societies. The period covered by the years 1966 to 1974 was a time of considerable intellectual ferment in Schillebeeckx's life: ferment because he met people in turmoil. In terms of charting the genesis of this ferment, 1966 is a crucial time. During that year he began to teach hermeneutics in Nijmegen's university. By the late 1960s, his thought had become decidedly hermeneutical. We shall see what this means shortly. His first visit to the United States of America also took place in 1966.

Experiences in Nijmegen and North America played a considerable part in altering the shape of Schillebeeckx's theology. During and after his visits to North America in 1966, and again in 1967, he became profoundly unsettled by what he interpreted as a pervasive crisis of faith undergone among people living in secularized pluralistic cultures such as the United States. This crisis involved two central difficulties: pluralism and historical change. In North America he witnessed a kind of supermarket of conflicting theological and philosophical views. In the midst of presuppositional pluralism, he could not perceive an all-inclusively shared positive theory that could serve as a basis for speaking about faith.

In other words, how does a Christian talk sensibly about faith to a Marxist who might not understand Christian terminology? Before his travels Schillebeeckx had relied on one overriding source to speak about faith: an amalgam of Aquinas's insights (Thomism), historical *ressourcement*, and De Petter's phenomenology. Because of his travels he recognized that his Thomistic–De Petterian language could not serve as an easily intelligible and universally acceptable basis from which to explain the essential meaning of Christian faith. Rather than searching for a particular philosophical perspective to serve as a language for dialogue in a pluralistic world, he settled upon the negative experience of human suffering. He proffered the view that all human beings suffer in one way or another. Hence, what faith in God and Christ might mean may be explored in a universally accessible experiential context, namely, the ubiquitous reality of suffering. This is not altogether unrelated to John Henry Newman's question: 'If one does not find God in the vicissitudes of life, where, then, will one find him?'[8]

After his journeys through the United States, and after his researches into hermeneutics, Schillebeeckx became much more aware of what he had learned with Chenu, that is to say, that all human knowledge is constrained by a historical context. It is not possible for humans to assume a view of things (a *pensée de survol*) outside the confines of history, or to imagine that there is some kind of supra-historical vantage point to which they might repair in order to view the entirety of history's meaning. Once it is conceded that humankind is hidebound by its historical particularity, that human knowledge is inherently perspectival because it is historically contextualized, and that the course of history is still unfolding, then any claim to achieve a purely theoretical, philosophical grasp of a totality of meaning is clearly constrained. Recognizing all this, Schillebeeckx emphasized that there is a correlation between human images of God, humankind, and the world. If one of these poles or images changes, then the other two will also be affected. During his visits abroad, and after reading hermeneutics and sociological analyses of secularization, Schillebeeckx became more aware of a new image of humankind and the world at large in American and European secularized societies. That image was focused on the future and not on the past. It understood human existence as a project bent on establishing an improved existence for humankind in a future world. The crisis of faith noted by Schillebeeckx involved a clash between the new future-directed understanding of humanity and the world on the one hand, and on the other hand, older theological language and concepts that spoke of God's transcendence in terms of, and on the basis of, concepts formulated in the context of experiences that no longer exist.

Faced with a clash between older images of God and newer anthropologies, Schillebeeckx searched for a new image of God and a reinterpretation of Christian faith that would gel with new future-oriented understandings of humanity and its world. The image he eventually found and formulated was of God as humankind's future. He began to speak of God in a new way as the future of humankind: God is 'The One Who Comes' (hence the title of GFM). This so-called new image of God is actually a rediscovery of an ancient biblical image: God is humanity's future, and its promise. The future-oriented society of which Schillebeeckx speaks was analysed by Ernst Bloch (1885–1977) who published his *Das Prinzip Hoffnung* (Eng. trans. *The Principle of Hope*, 1986) in 1959. Bloch's work was avidly scrutinized by Jürgen Moltmann (b. 1926) who began to interpret Bloch's secular eschatology (discourse on final, ultimate things in the future) in terms of a Christian eschatology. Schillebeeckx also read Bloch, and like Moltmann, placed his theology under the umbrella of eschatology.

To speak of God in terms of the future is to recognize four-squarely that the plenitude of God's transcendence (otherness) lies in the future. Therefore, while human history continues, it is impossible to find or know God exclusively from the vantage point of a historically localized and particular theory. By definition, the future cannot be elucidated theoretically; it can only be anticipated practically in actions that seek to determine the features the future might eventually assume. This line of argument explains why Schillebeeckx in the late 1960s began to speak so much about praxis. Bluntly stated, praxis is an action indivisibly linked to and guided by a theory. If God's very nature is to oppose all that is inhuman, then traces of God thus imagined might conceivably be glimpsed above all in forms of praxis that seek to bring about a more human existence in the future by practically resisting all that thwarts human development in the present.

Another major reason why Schillebeeckx's theology came to rely on a language of praxis has to do with suffering. Like the future, suffering is not ultimately explicable in theoretical terms. Schillebeeckx argues, correctly in my judgement, that there is no theory which adequately accounts to everyone's satisfaction for the existence of suffering, especially unmerited suffering, in a supposedly divine creation. The best response to suffering is to attempt to resist or alleviate it if at all possible. While suffering can certainly be pondered from abstract and theoretical vantage points, these should ideally follow, so the argument runs, in the wake of practical resistance (see GAU, p. 149).

THE ANCILLARY DISCIPLINES OF SCHILLEBEECKX'S LATER THEOLOGY

One might disagree with Schillebeeckx's reading of his historical situation in the mid-1960s, but the point to be retained at all costs here is that he was under the impression that a good many Christians at that time regarded a great deal of Christianity's time-honoured language as antiquarian and meaningless in secularized, pluralistic cultures intent on moulding the future with the aid of science, industry and technology.

Feeling 'an almost feverish sense of urgency', to use Schillebeeckx's own phrase, he attempted to reinterpret faith for the benefit of those who no longer shared older understandings of human and cosmic existence (see GFM p. 169). I have already listed the main sources he used in his feverish reinterpretation, and here, for the purposes of gaining a ready access to the major contours of his theology, I shall limit myself to describing the significance of some of the more consequential sources. We have noted previously the prevalence of positivism in the nineteenth century and of phenomenology in the first half or so of the twentieth century. Apart from phenomenology, there were four other more philosophical sources that Schillebeeckx engaged in his programme of reinterpreting the meaning of faith. These sources were hermeneutics, ordinary language philosophy, Critical Theory, and the work of Emmanuel Lévinas (b. 1905). If positivism sought to explain the nature and meaning of reality through empirical observation, phenomenology, as a non-empirical science, aimed to interpret meaning in terms of consciousness. Hermeneutics, on the other hand, discoursed on the historical genesis of meaning, while Critical Theory elaborated on how meaning is influenced, or distorted, by politics, culture, and economics. Ordinary language philosophy examined the mediation of meaning through the use of language, while Lévinas's work has explored meaning in terms of a philosophy of human solidarity among individuals.

Methodologically, these currents of thought are clearly distinguishable from the pre-contemporary philosophies that were focused on substance and assumed that the meaning and truth of something resides in itself prior to its association with other things. Phenomenology, hermeneutics, the philosophy of ordinary language, Critical Theory, and Lévinas's philosophy are all philosophies of relation. By that I mean that they interpret the meaning and truth of something in virtue of its association with other things or with a system of meaning apart from itself. And so, phenomenology highlights the intentional relation between a subjective interpreting consciousness and a world of objective things. Hermeneutics underscores the relation between text and interpreter. Philosophies of ordinary language underscore the structural relations between individual speech and systems of language. Critical Theory draws attention to the social relation obtaining between a human subject and its historical–political environment.[9] And finally, Lévinas concentrates on asymmetrical ethical relationships between human beings and commends the view that in face-to-face interpersonal relationships, one person commands a one-way ethical priority over the other.

One could well ask why Schillebeeckx assimilated postulates from the disciplines just mentioned as late as the 1960s. The origins of modern hermeneutics are frequently associated with Friedrich Schleiermacher (1768–1834) in the nineteenth century. Ordinary language philosophy was first developed in the 1950s, and Critical Theory initially made its presence felt in the 1920s. Nevertheless, it was particularly during the 1960s and 1970s that these disciplines underwent a recrudescence in European universities and were assimilated by academic theologians. A dialogue between Christian theologians and Marxist theorists was established in Europe in the 1960s. Three theologians in particular attended to new anti-positivist disciplines in concert with Schillebeeckx. Wolfhart Pannenberg (b. 1928) spoke of a totality of meaning in the future (see his *Offenbarung als Geschichte*, 1961; Eng. trans. *Revelation as History*, 1969). Jürgen Moltmann, to stress a point made above, expounded an eschatological counterpart (see his *Theologie der Hoffnung*, 1964; Eng. trans. *Theology of Hope*, 1967) to Ernst Bloch's advocacy of the utopian primacy of the future. And Johann Baptist Metz (b. 1928) published a political theology in 1966 (in his *Zur Theologie der Welt*; Eng. trans. *Theology of the World*, 1969) advocating the theological and epistemological significance of praxis. Both Metz and Moltmann participated in the Marxist–Christian dialogues of the 1960s.

(a) Hermeneutics

After Schillebeeckx began to teach hermeneutics to postgraduate students in Nijmegen's faculty of theology, he continued to do so until his retirement from the university. After he visited the United States he began a study of religious sociology and paid great attention to the phenomenon of secularization. His study of the sociological analysis of secularization may be regarded as an initial significant source for his effort to rethink Christian faith's primordial meaning. His gradually developing acquaintance with hermeneutics consolidated his new approach to interpreting faith in the light of secularization. A superabundance of philosophical assumptions at play in secularized societies had led him to eschew the possibility of interpreting faith on the basis of a particular philosophical school of thought. He began to reinterpret it instead, in the light of universally recognizable negative experiences of suffering.

Hermeneutics is the theory of interpretation (*ars interpretandi*) and especially of the interpretation of texts. It is a science that clarifies how texts are to be understood properly. It is an ancient discipline that was developed in a modern form by nineteenth- and twentieth-century German thinkers in the social context of a heightened sense of the historical nature of human reflection.[10]

Schillebeeckx evolved in his acquaintance with hermeneutics in three distinct stages. Firstly, he studied philosophical hermeneutics with special attention to the works of Hans-Georg Gadamer (b. 1900) and Paul Ricoeur as well as the theological hermeneutics of Rudolf Bultmann (1884–1976). Then he studied analytical philosophies of language and the so-called new hermeneutics of Gerhard Ebeling (b. 1912) and Ernst Fuchs (1903–83). Lastly, he attended to a more practical-critical hermeneutical school of thought associated with Critical Theory and, in particular, with the

German philosopher Jürgen Habermas (b. 1929). The all-important consequence of his appropriation of hermeneutics was his conclusion that the best way to keep faith alive is not a literal repetition of past texts but their reinterpretation in light of contemporary modes of thought. Biblical fundamentalism assumes that biblical texts are intelligible in themselves without attention to their cultural and historical contexts and that a process of interpretation is not required in order for them to be comprehended. Similarly, dogmatic fundamentalism argues that ecclesiastical dogmas are readily intelligible apart from their historical contexts. Schillebeeckx is now a markedly hermeneutical thinker maintaining that the meaning of any dogma needs to be interpreted in the light, not only of its historical setting, but also in relation to contemporary modes of experience and reflection.

(b) The philosophy of ordinary language

After the Enlightenment, many Western forms of philosophy concentrated on the human subject and its rationality. Phenomenology dwelt on consciousness, but it underestimated the significance of language in relation to consciousness. If the seventeenth, eighteenth, and nineteenth centuries witnessed a philosophical turn to the subject, as it were, the twentieth century heralded a resolute turn to language.

For the purposes of understanding Schillebeeckx's later theology it is helpful to consider his appropriation of what is called ordinary language philosophy, which is not to be confused with two earlier twentieth-century philosophies treating language: logical atomism and logical positivism. These last two are associated with, among others, the work of Bertrand Russell (1872–1970) and the younger Ludwig Wittgenstein (1889–1951). In Wittgenstein's more mature reflections on language, he confirmed a primary tenet of ordinary language philosophy according to which the meaning of language is closely connected with the way it is used. While philosophers such as Peter Strawson (b. 1919) and Gilbert Ryle (1900–76) have argued about the precise nature of the connection between linguistic usage and meaning, a distinguishing mark of ordinary language philosophy is the assertion that meaning is not prior to language as if words merely give form to a pre-existing intention or meaning. Rather, according to this view, meaning only becomes apparent at all in virtue of a pre-established and functioning language.

Whatever is to be thought of ordinary language philosophy, the primary upshot of Schillebeeckx's studies of language was his appreciation that meaning is mediated through the filter, so to speak, of linguistic structures and patterns.

(c) Critical Theory

Like phenomenology, Critical Theory is an amorphous current of thought with different adherents espousing diverse perspectives.

With Critical Theory and its philosophical antecedents, Western philosophy turned once again, but this time in the direction of society. In the twentieth century there have been three generations of exponents of Critical Theory working mostly in Germany and the United States of America. Critical Theory was initially developed in the Institute for Social Research chartered in the University of Frankfurt in 1923. The first generation of theorists worked there from 1923 to the late 1920s and in North America from where the Institute was directed during the 1930s and 1940s. It returned to Frankfurt in 1950. The second generation of Critical Theory is represented by Jürgen Habermas and his associates, and the third by his students and sympathizers.

From its beginnings, Frankfurt's Institute for Social Research was closely associated with Marxism. To be sure, it was the first explicitly Marxist institute of higher learning to be established in Germany. In 1917 a successful Marxist-inspired revolution was staged in Russia. In the 1920s, however, there were a number of unsuccessful Marxist-led social revolutions in Germany, Hungary and Italy. The first generation of Critical Theorists, philosophers such as Max Horkheimer (1895–1973) and Theodor Wiesengrund Adorno (1903–69), explained the failures of the social revolutions over and against classical Marxism, which they regarded as blinkered in its attempt to explain the driving forces of history mainly in terms of economic production. Critical Theory, then, is an expression of Western Marxism. Its first generation of exponents espoused a new form of Marxism by arguing that in order for societies to be radically altered politically, and in order for revolutions to succeed, then movements for revolution need to examine concepts such as culture, ideology, socialism, consciousness, and subjectivity. Expressed otherwise, whereas classical (orthodox) Marxism focused on the politics of class struggle and economic history, Western Marxism dwelt more on culture and ideology.[11] In the long run, Critical Theory in its initial form was distinguishable from more traditional social theories by its reliance on a wider array of intellectual disciplines. From its inception it probed fields such as economics, politics, culture, and aesthetics in order to expound a critique of dominators who hold others in a state of political, social and economic subjugation. In a word, Critical Theory is a theory of liberation for those who are socially oppressed.

With regard to Schillebeeckx's attention to Critical Theory, three observations need to be made. First, his acquaintance with it is largely confined to a reading of second-generation Western Marxists. Second, he is selective in the ideas he culls from the Theory: he takes issue with Western Marxism as well as learning from it. Thirdly, his attention to Critical Theory in no way implies that he rejected the fundamental insights of either phenomenology or philosophical hermeneutics. Critical Theory inclined him to consider the question of the meaning of faith in association with social and political questions.

The really important figure looming in Schillebeeckx's under-standing of Critical Theory is Habermas. A word of caution needs to be entered here, because, like Schillebeeckx's theology, Habermas's philosophy is a continually evolving project of inquiry. All of which is to say that Schillebeeckx's acquaintance with Habermas is very largely confined to the latter's early work enunciated in three books: *Theorie und Praxis* (1963; Eng. trans. *Theory and Practice*, 1974), *Erkenntnis und Interesse* (1968; Eng. trans. *Knowledge and Human Interests*, 1972), and *Zur Logik der Sozialwissenschaften* (1969; Eng. trans. *On the Logic of the Social Sciences*, 1988).

After reading Critical Theory Schillebeeckx came to the con-clusion that a purely theoretical, philosophical hermeneutics is untenable because understanding can be severely frustrated by social and political structures. If such is the case, then hermeneutics must have an emancipative, practical and critical interest that fosters human freedom and understanding. In order to link a Christian understanding of faith with social and political exigencies, Schillebeeckx turned especially to Habermas's early exposition of Critical Theory.

Habermas's early work emphasized that all knowledge is deter-mined by interest. His emphasis is an affront to positivism which maintains that science can be purely objective and free of mitigating subjective interests. Even so, Habermas demarcated three types of science each with a different covert interest: empirical sciences seek control; humane sciences are bent on communication between different parties; while socially critical sciences seek freedom for social subjects. In all three types of science, Habermas posited an inner bond between praxis and theory, in which the former deter-mines the latter.

Schillebeeckx professes that Critical Theory is fired by the assumption that for the first time in history human beings now have the scientific and technological means to enable themselves to deter-mine the course their history will take. Moreover, the Theory asserts that coercive social structures are changeable. Hence the signi-ficance of the precedence accorded to praxis: the only way for coercive and oppressive religious, political, or ethical theories to be overcome is from a starting point of praxis. All this is highly reminiscent of Karl Marx's oft-quoted dictum according to which, to paraphrase, philosophers have always interpreted the world while the point is to change it (see his *Theses on Feuerbach* (1845), especially the eleventh). For Marx, knowledge has its origins in praxis. Schillebeeckx, by adopting Critical Theory's understanding of itself as the self-consciousness of an emancipative, critical praxis, began in the late 1960s and early 1970s to define theology as 'the critical self-consciousness of Christian praxis in the world and the church'.[12]

A consequence of Schillebeeckx's attention to Critical Theory was that his reinterpretation of faith became more politically responsible, eschatologically orientated, and resolutely attentive to suffering. As far as I am aware, he has never made a systematic study of the works of Walter Benjamin (1892–1940). He has, however, closely analysed to momentous effect the major works of Theodor Adorno. Adorno was a close associate of Benjamin. It is at least arguable that through Adorno, by a process of osmosis, Schillebeeckx became more aware of a way of speaking of universality in connection with particularity. For Benjamin, and for the later Schillebeeckx, the universal can only be grasped within the particular. With Adorno, Schillebeeckx came across a philosophy profoundly preoccupied by human suffering. A major oversight, indeed questionable trait, of Schillebeeckx's early theology, written as it was in the immediate trail of World War II, is that it did not explore intently the theological ramifications of human suffering. Adorno and other Western Marxists were much more forthright in drawing attention to the portentous significance of suffering, especially as it is encapsulated in the symbol of Auschwitz: 'After Auschwitz, our feelings resist any claim of the positivity of existence as sanctimonious, as wronging the victims; they balk at squeezing any kind of sense, however bleached, out of the victims' fate'.[13]

(d) North American pragmatism

Schillebeeckx rarely mentions North American philosophical pragmatism in his writings, but when he does, he provides a vital clue explaining his reformulation of Christian faith in terms of action and theory rather than in terms of pure theory. After he visited the United States he admitted that he had previously misunderstood pragmatism as promoting the idea that whatever is expedient or useful is true. His encounter with North American philosophical pragmatism led him to revise his earlier misunderstanding that pragmatism espouses an outright expediency, and to perceive it instead as a recognition that truth, thinking, and action are inseparably connected.[14]

(e) The philosophy of Emmanuel Lévinas

With regard to Schillebeeckx's attention to Lévinas's philosophy, my sole purpose at this stage is simply to underscore that once Schillebeeckx encountered a plurality of philosophical world-views in secularized societies, he relied on Lévinas's ethical philosophy of solidarity among people in face-to-face encounters as a tool for expatiating on the meaning of faith in the context of human experiences of suffering. In the 1960s and 1970s, Lévinas's philosophy was rather more prominent in Europe than in Anglophone countries.

CONTEMPORARY BIBLICAL STUDIES

So much for the subsidiary resources employed by Schillebeeckx in his later theological project. A brief word now, about his attention to biblical studies. Quite sophisticated philological and exegetical techniques for interpreting the Bible were developed in Europe over the past two hundred years, most notably by Protestant scholars. Roman Catholic acceptance of the results of modern scientific scrutiny of the Bible lagged behind Protestant research until the early stages of the twentieth century. In the early 1960s, it was still possible to read works by Catholic dogmatic theologians that largely ignored the findings of biblical research in favour of philosophical argumentation or historical dissections of dogmatic decrees. In his later writings Schillebeeckx sounded once more the battle-cry of Le Saulchoir: 'back to the sources'. But he did so with a decisive difference. While French Dominicans had directed his attention to mediaeval sources, and Jesuits to even more ancient documents, the social upheavals he witnessed in the mid-1960s impelled him to reinterpret faith by returning to the most significant Jewish–Christian text of all, namely, the Bible; and to interpret it in the light of contemporary experiences.

CONCLUSION

This chapter has been somewhat laden with technical terms that crop up frequently in Schillebeeckx's publications. While it may be irksome to plough through his different non-theological sources and terminology, the effort to do so assists appreciably an attempt to understand why his theological arguments and discussions assume the form they do. His sources have been explained in the briefest of fashions here. For all that has been said about them, a great deal more has been left unsaid. But even a selective overview of his intellectual evolution indicates just how earnestly he has attempted as a Christian thinker to elucidate the meaning of faith in the changing social and historical circumstances in which he has found himself. Having considered some of his more significant resources, we turn now to a survey of the various publications in which he employs his ancillary disciplines to expound Christianity's identity.

Notes

1 Consult JWC, pp. 62–3; GM, pp. 18–40; and III, p. xv.
2 See Edward Schillebeeckx, 'God, the Living One', *New Blackfriars* 62: 735 (1981), pp. 357–70 (pp. 362–5).
3 See Edward Schillebeeckx, 'The religious and the human ecumene' in Marc H. Ellis and Otto Maduro (eds), *The Future of Liberation Theology: Essays in Honor of Gustavo Gutiérrez* (Maryknoll, NY: Orbis Books, 1989), pp. 177–88 (esp. p. 184).
4 For an explanation of what Schillebeeckx means by a situated freedom and for his references to Gusdorf, see GM, pp. 41, 249, 258, n. 1; pp. 280–1; and pp. 285–6. For an illustration of the way Schillebeeckx has retained the nucleus of Gusdorf's anthropology while at the same time amplifying it, see the former's article, 'Questions on Christian

salvation of and for man' in David Tracy with Hans Küng and Johann B. Metz (eds), *Toward Vatican III: The Work That Needs to Be Done* (New York: Seabury/Concilium, 1978), pp. 27–44 (pp. 30–40). This article builds on material previously published in II, pp. 734–43. While accepting postulates gleaned from atheistic existentialist anthropologies, Schillebeeckx also maintains that a human being is the primary symbol of the divine in history. Hence his expression 'The human story of God' (the subtitle of III).

5   See T. M. [= Ted] Schoof, *A Survey of Catholic Theology: 1800–1970* (Paramus, NJ: Paulist Newman Press, 1970), pp. 108–11, esp. p.111.

6   Edmund Husserl, *Formale und Transzendentale Logik* (The Hague: Martinus Nijhoff, 1974), p. 239.

7   See Paul Natorp, 'On the objective and subjective grounding of knowledge', *Journal of the British Society for Phenomenology* 12 (1981), pp. 245–66 (p. 248).

8   Quoted, without an exact reference, in GM, p. 219.

9   I am indebted here to the work of Richard Kearney, *Modern Movements in European Philosophy* (Manchester: Manchester University Press, 1986), p. 2.

10 See Galye Ormiston and Alan D. Schrift (eds), *The Hermeneutic Tradition: From Ast to Ricoeur* (Albany, NY: State University of New York Press, 1990), esp. p. 11.

11 See Douglas Kellner, *Critical Theory, Marxism and Modernity* (Cambridge and Oxford: Polity Press, 1989), p. 12; and Tom Bottomore, *The Frankfurt School* (Chichester and London: Ellis Horwood and Tavistock Publications, 1984), p. 18.

12 UF, p. 154. See p. 142 as well.

13 Theodor W. Adorno, *Negative Dialectics* (London: Routledge & Kegan Paul, 1990), p. 361.

14 See Edward Schillebeeckx, 'Catholic life in the United States', *Worship* 42 (1968), pp. 134–49 (p. 147).

4

Works and themes

One useful way of pinpointing the central preoccupation of an outstanding thinker is to pose the question: Who or what is this thinker arguing against; and what is this thinker arguing for? In Schillebeeckx's case, there is one particular conviction with which he has crossed swords since the beginning of his academic career. From the 1940s onwards he has disputed the notion that Christianity thwarts human freedom. In modern times, and especially since the seventeenth-century European Enlightenment, Christianity has faced an unnerving foe in Europe and its former colonies. That foe has been neither a particular nation nor a cohort of irreligious intellectuals, but rather, a generally pervasive suspicion that to profess Christian faith is to enter into an irrational vassalage to out-worn understandings of human existence. Considered as a whole, Schillebeeckx's theological output is an unflinching apologia for Christianity understood as a path to freedom, a path initially hewn, so the argument evolves, by Jesus of Nazareth. This chapter outlines the major works and predominant themes of Schillebeeckx's output. I make no attempt in what follows to tabulate his several hundred publications. I simply list the more significant ones and briefly comment on their reigning preoccupations. But before doing so, it is instructive to consider the question of freedom that is a major intellectual interlocutor to which Schillebeeckx's earliest set of publications, and indeed his entire body of writings, respond.

THE QUESTION OF FREEDOM

In the previous chapter we had occasion to take note of Immanuel Kant's programmatic essay 'What is Enlightenment?', in which he dared his readers to use their reason and to think for themselves. To repeat a familiar issue, he declared that the motto of the Enlightenment was to encourage people to have the courage to use their own reason: *Sapere aude* ('Dare to be wise'). He observed that cowardice and laziness keep a large part of humankind in self-incurred dependence on the direction or authority of others. For Kant and philosophers of his ilk, one should not defer to ecclesiastical authorities as a wellspring for the revelation of truth. One should employ one's reason. For the Enlightenment, to generalize, there is only one reliable, genuine, authoritative form of authority and touchstone for truth, and that is the knowledge gained by an autonomous rational subject.

I re-emphasize Kant's call to freedom from tutelage through the use of reason, for two reasons. First, to draw attention to the way freedom became one of the more salient preoccupations and themes of Western philosophy from the eighteenth to the twentieth century. And second, to indicate that Schillebeeckx describes himself quite explicitly as someone who stands in the tradition of the Enlightenment. He has not sought merely to assimilate aspects of Kant's critiques of reason. He has also met the latter's challenge to refer the contents of thought back to living experience. Resonating Kant's famous dictum that thoughts without contents are void (*Critique of Pure Reason*, B75), Schillebeeckx frequently notes the necessity to bridge a gap between thought and experience beleaguering, so he thinks, contemporary Christian circles: 'Christian belief is indeed empty, powerless and irrelevant if it has no relationship to our experience as human beings'.[1] Kant's thesis that the human mind actively interprets sensory data in terms of concepts, and his postulate that theological affirmations about God cannot be buffered by arguments based on a putatively pure form of reason, are amply evident in Schillebeeckx's works.[2] De Petter had taught Schillebeeckx the importance of examining Kant's theory of reason for the purposes of superseding a naïvely realistic theory of knowledge. After Schillebeeckx's philosophical turnabout, he came to correct Kant's assumptions by theorizing about knowledge in relation to a theory of society. Clearly, Schillebeeckx has favourably received some of the more important insights of Kantian philosophy. Moreover, he regards the hard-won political gains of the French Revolution in a receptive light, its violent excesses notwithstanding. Yet while he regards the Enlightenment as a positive tradition and shares its interests in rationality and freedom, he also abjures its very constrained notion of freedom: 'My freedom at the expense of your freedom'. He rejects what he calls its 'bourgeois Christ', that is, its identification of middle-class values and concepts with the Christ of Christian faith. For Schillebeeckx, Enlightenment ideas about freedom were limited to the sphere of middle-class values and did not encompass freedom for the socially outcast.[3] Thus, he is neither a naïve epistemological realist, nor a naïve *Aufklärer* or blinkered devotee of the Enlightenment. He realizes full well that one needs to be enlightened about the Enlightenment.

As a correction to the Enlightenment's lopsided notion of freedom, Schillebeeckx's theology relies on what he calls a second 'positive tradition', namely Christianity: the tradition of Jesus of Nazareth and the entire movement that followed him.[4] Therefore, it comes as no surprise to find Schillebeeckx speaking of Jesus as 'The Free Man' and of his life as 'The Way to Freedom' (GAU, pp. 1 and 45–52). In contraposition to the idea that Christianity stifles freedom, Schillebeeckx's impelling intellectual fervency, evident in the first set of articles he wrote, has been to assert that Christianity magnifies human freedom, especially the freedom of those kept in tutelage by a supposedly enlightened middle or upper class.

To speak of Christianity's unnerving enemy in terms of the idea that Christianity suffocates freedom might appear overly rhetorical and hyperbolic, but it is as well to recognize that the general cultural and political context in which Schillebeeckx began to publish his thoughts, in 1945, was one of a near complete social collapse where confidence in the tenets of Christian faith had been inexorably eroded by the horrors of war. Schillebeeckx began to publish in crisis-ridden circumstances. Christianity had not been able to preserve Europe from internecine world wars between nominally Christian nations. Far worse than that, it is at least arguable that a particular Christian misunderstanding of the religio-socio-political causes of Jesus' death, contributed, during World War II, to a fanatical persecution of Jews, speciously and simplistically interpreted as the descendants of Jesus' persecutors. As that war drew to a close, Belgium, the Netherlands, Luxembourg, France and Germany were extensively bombed and ravaged by opposing armies. After the industrialization of Europe in the nineteenth century, hopes had been high there that human beings could build a new world order with the aid of science and technology, and not especially with the assistance of Christianity. The result? In a word, the bedlam of warfare. After 1945, Belgium was deeply unsettled by a number of serious social problems. To begin with, there was an intense debate in the country about the relation between the Belgian king, Leopold III, and the Germans. The king eventually ceded powers to one of his sons in 1950. Secondly, Flemish people who had collaborated with the Germans were severely ostracized. And finally, there was considerable internal debate in Flanders as to the autonomy or otherwise of Catholic schools.

Schillebeeckx's thought was first published in the immediate setting of an embattled and exhausted Belgium; and in the broader circumstances of a war-torn Europe. To maintain that Christianity could herald freedom in such a state of affairs would require more than rhetorical declamation. From where could deliverance from the inanities of war come? Whence hope and freedom? Schillebeeckx began to enunciate his response to questions such as these in a set of articles that he published before he went to live in France in 1946. Over the past five decades he has expressed his thought in four principal forms: articles for various journals; books, which are frequently collections of previously published essays; collections of occasional addresses and sermons; and lastly, the unpublished monographs of lectures and conferences. Most of his articles have appeared in five different Dominican journals: *Kultuurleven* ('Cultural Life'); *Ons Geloof* ('Our Faith'); *Tijdschrift voor Geestelijk Leven* ('Journal for the Spiritual Life'); *Tijdschrift voor Theologie* ('Journal for Theology'); and *De Bazuin* ('The Trumpet'). The first three had their origins in Belgium; the others were edited from Nijmegen.

It is not without significance that Schillebeeckx first began to write in *Kultuurleven*, since this was an organ used by Flemish Dominicans to develop a theology of culture, that is, to examine the way Christianity could function at the time in the cultural context of Belgium. With *Kultuurleven*, Schillebeeckx found an outlet for developing the interest he took over from Chenu, namely, the concentration on the interplay and co-dependence between nature and supernature, or, expressed differently, between that which is finite and infinite. But the interplay was examined in terms of the interrelation between the world and the Church. Be it noted, though, that both interplays — nature/supernature and world/Church — are transpositions of Schillebeeckx's architectonic intellectual absorption: the intersection between universality and particularity.

THE SIX ARTICLES OF 1945

Of the six articles that Schillebeeckx published in 1945, three appeared in *Kultuurleven*, one in *Ons Geloof*, and two in *Tijdschrift voor Geestelijk Leven*. A perusal of these essays is highly illuminating. Not only do they give evidence of the major preoccupations of Schillebeeckx's career. They also evince theological principles or conceptual grids that have remained operative in his works ever since.

The first text Schillebeeckx ever published appeared in January 1945. It was entitled 'Schepsel-besef als grondslag van ons geestelijk leven' ('The sense of being a creature as the basis for our spiritual life'), and was contained in the first volume of the *Tijdschrift voor Geestelijk Leven* ever to be published (vol. 1, pp. 15–43). Four features of the article are worthy of note. First, it speaks of God as a sovereign Creator (p. 16) and of everything that human beings possess as a gift from the Creator (p. 23). In so doing it announces an understanding of God that Schillebeeckx retains to this day (see III, pp. 228–46). Second, it addresses the question of freedom. Schillebeeckx argues that Christians are endowed with an authentic autonomy which stems from their self-awareness as creatures of a sovereign Creator (pp. 17, 18, and 23). He argues his case in dialogue with humanistic and existentialist philosophies, and with particular allusion to Friedrich Nietzsche (1844–1900), who was capable of sarcastic and inflammatory criticism of Christianity. In the third place, the article betrays an interest in the Flemish mysticism of Jan van Ruusbroec (1293–1381) (pp. 23 and 31). The same mystic is referred to in Schillebeeckx's most recent major book, *Church: The Human Story of God* (pp. 70–1). Fourthly, the article is clearly directed to a Roman Catholic audience. This feature is distinguishable from Schillebeeckx's latest work, which does not presuppose an avowedly Catholic readership.

The next month, in February 1945, Schillebeeckx published another essay, called 'Technische Heilstheologie' ('Technical theology of salvation') in the Flemish journal *Ons Geloof* (vol. 27, pp. 49–60). The essay is essentially an exposition of Aquinas's approach to theology, but encapsulates the major themes of Schillebeeckx's entire theological project. We have had occasion above to remark that during the mid-1960s Schillebeeckx found himself trying to reinterpret Christian faith for those disillusioned and disabused by secularization, pluralism, and historical consciousness. The principle he clung to in his discourses on what guarantees that a reinterpretation of faith conforms to primordial Christian faith-proclamations, is a principle gleaned from Aquinas and quoted in the article 'Technical theology of salvation' (p. 52). That principle runs like this: 'The act of the believer does not terminate at a statement (of faith) but at the reality ("actus credentis non terminatur ad enuntiabile sed ad rem").' In other words, one believes in God and not in statements about God. That which guarantees continuity in substance between ancient and new-born interpretations of faith is the object believed in, that is, the reality of God. This is a capital conclusion that underwrites all of Schillebeeckx's subsequent attempts to interpret the meaning of Christian faith.[5]

That Thomas Aquinas is the lodestar for a good deal of Schillebeeckx's thought is further evidenced in the way the latter defines theology in terms highly reminiscent of the former. In the essay presently under consideration, Aquinas is frequently cited as Schillebeeckx describes theology in the following manner:

(a) Theology is, and always will be, a scientific reflection concerning faith (p. 59);

(b) Insofar as theology is a reflection on faith, its nature is determined by faith's structure (p. 51);

(c) The structure of faith is such that the God of salvation (*Deus salutaris*) is its object (p. 52);

(d) Consequently, an act of faith terminates in the reality of God regarded as the First Truth who brings salvation (*Veritas prima salutaris*) and not in propositions about God (pp. 52–3);

(e) Granted that God is salvation itself, then Christ may be understood as the means to salvation. Hence, the two basic truths giving faith its foundation are the mystery of the Trinity on the one hand, and the humanity of Christ on the other (p. 54); and finally,

(f) Theology is technical in that it involves reflection which is methodologically conducted, systematically planned, and critically justified (pp. 56 and 59).

This last point explains why the word 'technical' is used in the essay's title.

To draw threads together, it could be said that while the first article Schillebeeckx released in 1945 announces his theme of creation, the essay on theology as a technical science discloses an attendant theme, which is to say, salvation. His theology is frequently interpreted as a soteriology, that is, as a theory of salvation. His later work regularly speaks of 'salvation-in-Jesus-from-God' (*heil-in-Jezus van Godswege*), a stock phrase for defining the central interest of Christianity:

> One is a Christian if one is persuaded that final salvation-from-God is disclosed in the person of Jesus and that this basic conviction gives rise to the community or fellowship of grace. . . .[6]

And so, the notion that Christian faith is inherently soteriological, or concerned with salvation, is clearly presaged in the essay of February 1945 in which Schillebeeckx posits a (Creator) God as the content of salvation, and the humanity of Jesus Christ as the means for recognizing that salvation. Viewing the two essays under consideration here synoptically, one finds the theocentric focus of his thought discussed in relation to his Christocentric focus, and both foci examined in connection with the themes of creation and salvation. As early as 1945, Schillebeeckx expressed his theological vision in a nutshell: God the Creator, through the act of creation, initiates a history of salvation and constitutes the content of salvation which is mediated to human beings through Jesus Christ. Very much the same vision sustains his book *Church: The Human Story of God.*

February 1945 witnessed the publication of yet another article by Schillebeeckx, the first in a set of three interconnected essays. All of them bear on the Church/world polarity under the guise of a discussion of Christianity's association with contemporary European societies. The first in the series was entitled 'Christelijke Situatie' ('The Christian situation') and appeared in the Flemish journal *Kultuurleven* (vol. 12, pp. 82–95). The text refers to Nietzsche proclaiming 'the death of God', and broaches the topic of a godless and religionless humanity (pp. 83–4). Schillebeeckx's early work designates religious apostasy and atheism as the most significant phenomena of his time (see GM, p. 34). In 'The Christian situation' he attempts to describe a confrontation between Christianity and a seemingly humanistic and godless culture. The second text in the set bears the title 'Christelijke Situatie: Grondbeginselen voor een Cultuurtheologie' ('The Christian situation: foundations for a theology of culture'). It was published in May 1945, in *Kultuurleven*, vol. 12, pp. 229–42. It continues to sketch an apparent clash between Christianity and twentieth-century humanism. The third article has a revealing title: 'Christelijke Situatie: III. — Naar een Oplossing: Bovennatuurlijk Exclusivisme' ('The Christian situation: III. — Towards a solution: supernatural exclusivism'). It appeared in November 1945, once again in *Kultuurleven* (vol. 12, pp. 585–611). As its title indicates, the article strives to suggest a solution to a perceived rift between Christianity and the contemporary European humanistic cultures in which it is enmeshed. It argues in effect that European humanism is really the aftermath and reverse side of a one-sided absorption with supernaturè among Christians ('supernatural exclusivism') to the disparagement of secular existence (p. 607). While speaking of supernatural exclusivism, Schillebeeckx returns once more to the theme of freedom by asserting that, in view of existentialist humanistic interests in freedom, Catholics need not regard themselves as totally bereft of freedom. On the contrary, they have received a freedom from God on the basis of which they may assume secular endeavours in present-day circumstances. In relation to their cultures, contemporary Christians need not succumb to either a cultural humanism or pessimism, but, on the contrary, may live according to a priority higher than humanism's, namely, the kingdom of God preached by Jesus Christ (ibid.). Apart from the recurrent interest in presenting Christianity as a way to freedom, the essay treating supernatural exclusivism is arresting because it bespeaks a confidence in a primary tenet of Thomism, namely, that secularity is not to be discredited: the world is meant to be secular and profane simply because the world is neither God nor on a par with God. Much later in his career, Schillebeeckx evinced the same kind of, as he called it, 'Thomistic acceptance of the worldliness of the world' (III, p. 205).

The sixth article that Schillebeeckx penned in 1945 appeared in the Flemish journal of spiritual concerns *Tijdschrift voor Geestelijk Leven* (vol. 1, 309–18). It bore the title 'De Akte van Volmaakte Liefde' ('The act of perfect love'). It treats one of the more salient of Schillebeeckx's theological interests, which is to say, it broaches the not uncomplicated matter of how God is known by human beings. We have observed above that Schillebeeckx relies on Aquinas's axiom that even though God's essence cannot be known, it is at least possible for human beings to perceive something of God through the divine manifestation which is creation. In 'The act of perfect love' Schillebeeckx makes exactly the same point. He opines that God is not immediately accessible to human beings, but can only be known in nature, that is, indirectly through creation.

THE SACRAMENTAL ECONOMY OF SALVATION

Schillebeeckx continued to publish clusters of essays in successive years after 1945. Indeed he is primarily a theological essayist, because even his larger monographs frequently contain material previously published as articles in journals. Between 1947 and 1957, it will be recalled, Schillebeeckx acted as Master of Dominican Students in Louvain. In that charge he was responsible for supervising the spiritual development of the students. His supervision is reflected in his articles, a large proportion of which are devoted to themes such as sacramental life, the mystery of God's love, the rosary, and the Holy Spirit — all matters of concern for young Dominicans at the time.

In 1952, however, Schillebeeckx published his first major monograph, called *De Sacramentele Heilseconomie* ('The Sacramental Economy of Salvation').[7] This book is the revised form of the first part of the dissertation that earned its author the degree of Doctor in Theology from Le Saulchoir in 1951. It is a work of nearly seven hundred pages, and if any publication in Schillebeeckx's corpus reveals his masterly command of Christian tradition, then it is this one. The text is liberally spiced with references to Church Fathers and mediaeval theologians. The sub-title of the book further describes its characteristics: 'A theological reflection on St Thomas's teaching on sacraments in the light of tradition and the current sacramental problematic'. In the early stages of the book (p. v) Schillebeeckx indicates that it was written for students as a substitute for Neo-Scholastic manuals of sacramental theology. The word 'economy' in its title requires explanation since it is used in an entirely different way today to refer mainly to monetary matters. In the Middle Ages, however, and much earlier among Greek-speaking Christian theologians, economy was understood in another way as a discourse on salvation. For mediaeval thinkers, theology (*theologia*) was distinguished from economy (*oikonomia*). While theology, thus construed, concentrated on the internal life of the Godhead, economy dealt with God's saving activity in human history. In discussing the salvation wrought by God in the world, economy attended to the Church, sacraments, and Christ.

De Sacramentele Heilseconomie has never been translated. In essence it was an exercise in the theological *ressourcement* that Schillebeeckx had learned at Le Saulchoir, since, after examining Aquinas's doctrine on sacraments, he undertakes an extended survey of the historical context, prehistory and subsequent history of the doctrine in correspondence with other sacramental teachings. The book contains an analysis of sacramental debates at the sixteenth-century Council of Trent (pp. 185–98) and reviews attempts to renew sacramental theology in the twentieth century (pp. 207–35). Methodologically, the work is dogmatic, which is to say, its primary source and starting point is an examination of ecclesiastical dogmas and teachings. Even so, it is important to record that Schillebeeckx's dogmatic method always attempted to relate classical Christian doctrines to contemporary problems and understandings. Consequently, the survey of sacramental theory undertaken in the book is motivated by a desire to inquire as to how the meaning of sacraments might be comprehended adequately in current circumstances.

THE ENCOUNTER WITH GOD

The second part of Schillebeeckx's dissertation, dealing with more contemporary concerns, was never published. Nonetheless, in 1959, he released what was to become one of his most widely read works: called, translating the Dutch, *Christ the Sacrament of the Encounter with God*. In fact, this book is a revision of a text published the previous year with the title *The Encounter with Christ as a Sacrament of the Encounter with God*.[8] It is in this work that Schillebeeckx employs, to considerable effect, the existentialist notion of personal encounter as a way of expounding the meaning and significance of sacraments regarded in themselves as an economy of salvation. He defines a sacrament as 'a divine bestowal of salvation in an outwardly perceptible form which makes the bestowal manifest; a bestowal of salvation in historical visibility'. And again: a sacrament is

> primarily and fundamentally a personal act of Christ himself, which reaches and involves us in the form of an institutional act performed by a person in the Church who, in virtue of a sacramental character, is empowered to do so by Christ himself: an act *ex officio*. (CS, pp. 15 and 53)

Philosophically, *Christ the Sacrament* is an extraordinary mixture of two very different perspectives. The first is Platonic, that is, stemming from Plato (427–347 BCE); while the second is existentialist phenomenological anthropology. Plato taught that a 'High God' could not be directly involved with the material world. To explain how a perfect divine realm associates with an imperfect material world, he expounded the myth of a demiurge, an intermediary figure who passes between the two realms (see Plato's *Timaeus*). Hence the expression 'Platonic dualism': existence is divisible between a perfect divine realm of disembodied Ideas, and an imperfect realm of matter.

Schillebeeckx's early sacramental work reflects a similar dualistic structure. Which is not to say that he is a metaphysical dualist. As I have said, for Schillebeeckx, reality is unitary. Unlike Plato, he does not contend that finite material reality is totally set apart from a divine realm. Nonetheless, in his initial work on sacraments, his manner of speaking of Christ as a sacrament echoes Plato's schema of an intermediary figure passing between divine and corporeal realms. The Gospel according to John has a similar schema (John 1:1–18). But Schillebeeckx, apart from speaking of Christ in terms of an intermediary, or as the primordial sacrament of God, also engages the existentialist, phenomenological category of encounter: a person who encounters Christ in ecclesiastical sacraments thereby encounters God. The logic undergirding *Christ the Sacrament* is this: To encounter the Church is to encounter a sacrament of Christ who in turn is a sacrament of an encounter with God (see CS, pp. 13, 52–5, and 152). This idea of encounter fits in with the notion of a two-tiered cosmic order. *Christ the Sacrament* recurrently refers to an upward and downward movement: From above, God offers redeeming love to human beings by sending his Son, Jesus, down among them; and from below the Son is simultaneously 'the supreme realization of the response of human love to this divine offer' (p. 18). The primordial sacrament, Christ, is both the revelation of a redeeming God (downward thrust) and 'the supreme worshipper of the Father' (upward movement) (pp. 17–18). Were Schillebeeckx to re-examine the meaning of Christ in relation to the category of sacrament in the closing stages of the twentieth century, one wonders whether he would still retain the spatial metaphors of upward and downward movement to explain human encounter with God.

MARY, MOTHER OF THE REDEMPTION

Apart from writing on sacraments and spiritual theology for Dominican students, Schillebeeckx also wrote articles for a three-volume dictionary of theology (*Theologisch Woordenboek*) published between 1952 and 1958. Its second volume, printed in 1957, contains a lengthy article in which Schillebeeckx outlines a synthesis of theological reflection on Mary, the mother of Jesus. It was preceded in 1954 by the publication of Schillebeeckx's book called, translating the Dutch, *Mary, Christ's Most Beautiful Creation*, which was itself revised and re-issued in 1955 with the title *Mary, Mother of the Redemption*.[9] To summarize markedly, this book interprets the actions of Mary's life as having revelational significance in the history of salvation. If Christ is the principal figure in that history of salvation in which God is revealed then, for the early Schillebeeckx, Mary is second in importance to Christ. The book *Christ the Sacrament* spoke in terms of God's invitation (through Christ) and human beings' response to God in sacramental encounter. The 1955 book on Mary employs the same invitation/response scheme in which Mary is described as God's invitation or call to us (see the first chapter). And once more, Schillebeeckx's primary categories of creation and salvation are amply in evidence, but this time discussed in relation to Mary.

A fundamental difficulty with this book is that its theological claims on behalf of Mary are somewhat overblown. For example, Schillebeeckx speaks of Mary as a co-redemptrix (p. 79), that is, as someone who co-operates with Christ in the process of the redemption of humanity. The notion of Mary as co-redemptrix has mediaeval origins. St Bonaventure (1221–74) proffered the view that Mary participated in, as he put it, Christ's redemptive act on the cross. Even though Bonaventure clearly indicated that whatever is redemptive about Christ's death on the cross is unique to Christ, the notion of a co-redemptrix gradually developed in popular piety. In any case, many of the theological claims made about Mary, for example, that she is the mother of creation, the Church, or redemption, belong more appropriately in the first place, according to pre-mediaeval theological traditions, to the Holy Spirit. *Mary, Mother of the Redemption* also regards as unproblematical nineteenth- and twentieth-century reports concerning apparitions that Mary is believed to have made to certain individuals (pp. 146–52). The most that could be said about these so-called private revelations is that they are ambiguous and epiphenomenal in relation to the core of Christian faith. They could indeed be interpreted as manifestations of divine favour for particular persons, but reports of them could also be interpreted as betraying characteristics of hysterical hallucinations. But that is a matter for debate, and not of primary concern here.

In any event, it is worth noting that Schillebeeckx alters his early interpretation of Mary's significance, and explains the development of his Marian theology, in a very recent essay mentioned above in Chapter 1 (note 3 on p. 12): 'Mariologie, gisteren vandaag morgen' (1992).

THE INAUGURAL AND RETIREMENT LECTURES

At this juncture I should like to comment on two lectures delivered by Schillebeeckx at quite different stages in his life. The first was given to inaugurate his professorship in Nijmegen. The second was delivered on 11 February 1983, to commemorate his retirement from the university in Nijmegen and to recapitulate his primary theological interests. The inaugural address was entitled 'Op zoek naar de levende God' ('In search of the Living God'). By now, its themes are readily familiar: in the context of Dutch humanism, French existentialism, secularization, and modern atheism, Schillebeeckx restates his theocentric and Christocentric disposition by concluding that the incarnation of God in Christ is the specific source (*locus theologicus*) for humans in search of God to gain a point of access into the intratrinitarian divine mystery. Importantly, the speech prefigures two motifs that were to receive much more prominence in Schillebeeckx's later works: the incomprehensibility of suffering; and the notion that God is 'the One Who Comes' (*de komende God*).

The retirement lecture has never been published in its entirety. It compresses a great deal of reflection and summarizes the thought of Schillebeeckx's maturity. It is entitled 'The theological understanding of faith in the year 1983'. It returns to a pressing issue which overwhelmed its author in the 1960s: How is Christian faith to be transmitted and kept alive from one generation to the next? A highly significant feature of the speech is that it explains a major methodological change in Schillebeeckx's thinking. His earlier work sought to transmit and explain the meaning of faith on the basis of a *reditus ad fontes*, that is, by a return to examining classical texts and discussing them in the light of the present. The texts, though, were of paramount importance. By 1983, however, he had come to the conclusion that theology has two equally fundamental sources: texts from the past which record earlier experiences on the one hand, and contemporary experiences on the other. Hence, Schillebeeckx now speaks of a mutually critical correlation as a method for theology. In other words, he asserts that the meaning of faith is not warranted by a literal repristination or adroit interpretation of past texts. The meaning of faith is conveyed in a balance, or mutual critical correlation, between four factors: the original Christian message (tradition); its historical situation; current interpretations of faith; and their contexts. Thus, the identity of faith is identifiable when four poles are held in balance: the message and its situation, then and now. This idea is somewhat complex. It should be noted, in passing, that it was developed in an elaborate manner by the contemporary Swiss theologian Pierre Gisel.[10] At base, though, Schillebeeckx's methodological turnabout is a matter of balance and starting points. His early writings *began* with scrutinies of texts in their contexts. The meaning of the texts was then discussed in the light of present-day problems and awarenesses. His later writings analyse current experiences which are put on an equal footing with past texts as sources for theologizing. Rather than simply ransacking time-honoured texts for meaning, or merely attending to recent experiences, his later works have a bifocal vision, attending to both sources, held in a correlation, one to the other.

In addition to presenting a more elaborate view of theological methodology, the retirement speech explains the more distinctive features of Schillebeeckx's later theology. These are: the significance of narrative as a purveyor of meaning; the insistence that the hermeneutical (interpretative) problem for faith is not about relations between concepts, but between theory and praxis; and lastly, Christian theology is now much more aware of its situation in a world populated by many different religions and non-Christian cultures.[11]

PUBLICATIONS IN THE 1960s

Apart from a host of articles, the first large-scale work to be published by Schillebeeckx in the 1960s was a study of marriage called (in English) *Marriage: Human Reality and Saving Mystery*. It was meant to be a diptych, but only the first part was produced. The title of the study espouses the Thomistic confidence in the worldliness of the world. As the title of the book makes clear, Schillebeeckx concludes that marriage has meaning in and by itself, quite apart from any religious significance with which it might be invested. This stance is given a much sharper expression in one of Schillebeeckx's later offerings:

> Only a living relationship to God in Jesus Christ gives a religious significance both to marriage (and to other interpersonal human

relations) and to celibacy willingly adopted or forced on one by circumstances. I resolutely dispute that they have this religious significance in and of themselves. I therefore challenge both the twentieth-century religious mystification of marriage and the age-old Western Greek-Christian mystification of celibacy.[12]

Apart from the book on marriage, two works produced in 1966 are also worthy of our attention. The first interpreted the achievement of Vatican II by maintaining that the Council impelled Roman Catholic theology to become more biblical. The second was more daring in that it examined a matter which the bishops at the Council had been forbidden to discuss by the two Popes who presided successively over the Council. The question I am referring to concerned celibacy for clergymen. It is in the latter text that Schillebeeckx gives one of his most succinct explanations of the hermeneutical problem with which his theology began to grapple in 1966 and which was not overly evident in his works on Mary:

> Everywhere the hermeneutical problem keeps cropping up, in our biblical studies, theological speculations, and in every reflection upon the structures of the church. For human experience not only happens temporally; it also includes an awareness of time. Experienced time is the time which the human subject perceives as a being-in-the-world, but in his *awareness* of time man transcends it even though he cannot conquer it, or, as it were, put himself outside it. The course of our present life as it goes towards the future from out of the past has become the central problem in the world as well as the church. Becoming aware of this dimension *is* the present crisis, in the life of the church as well as in the economic, social, and political life of the world. It is obvious that our ideas of man, the world, and God that provided the basis for the structures, forms and expressions of the past have been fundamentally altered. But the forms and structures have remained; thus they have become all but incomprehensible and no longer viable for us. Insecurity prevails everywhere.[13]

Two further signally significant works of Schillebeeckx emanating from the 1960s were *God the Future of Man* (1969), a collection of lectures mentioned above that Schillebeeckx gave in North America; and two years before that a short treatise called (in the English translation) *The Eucharist* (1967), which is actually a compilation of two previously published articles. This second text is a reinterpretation of Aquinas's eucharistic doctrine, but in the light of Kant's distinction between reality and its phenomenological appearance, and Merleau-Ponty's work on the phenomenology of perception.[14]

THEOLOGICAL SOUNDINGS

In the early 1960s a group of British theologians, including Alec Vidler (b. 1899) and Harry Williams (b. 1919), who were centred on Cambridge, attempted to overcome what they regarded as English theology's excessive concentration on biblical doctrines. They attempted to explore new theological matter in dialogue with contemporary philosophies and psychologies. Not insignificantly, they published their investigations in a book called *Soundings*. From 1964, Schillebeeckx published soundings of his own in a five-volume series of books (*Theologische Peilingen* ('Theological Soundings')). For the main, the five works encompassed by the set gather together several of his articles published in preceding years. Their titles and guiding interests can be listed as follows:

(a) *Openbaring en Theologie* (1964; *Revelation and Theology*), dealing with scripture, tradition, and the nature of revelation, faith and theology;

(b) *God en Mens* (1965; *God and Man*), concentrating mainly on the problems posed for faith by humanism, existentialism, and secularization;

(c) *Wereld en Kerk* (1966; *World and Church*), focusing, as its title intimates, on the Church/world dialectic;

(d) *Zending van de Kerk* (1968; *The Mission of the Church*), incorporating several of the more consequential ideas of Vatican II; and finally,

(e) *Geloofsverstaan: interpretatie en kritiek* (1972; *The Understanding of Faith*), which contains the initial results of its author's studies in hermeneutics and philosophies of language.[15]

JESUS, THE STORY OF THE LIVING ONE

All of the books that Schillebeeckx published in the nine-year period before 1974 were collections of articles or lectures. It will be recalled that he perceived at Vatican II that Catholic theology had become more biblically orientated. Learning from the Council, and impelled in the midst of faith-crises, he set about in the late 1960s to pore over biblical studies in preparation for elaborating the meaning of Christian faith in a new way. In the first four years of the 1970s he pursued virtually no other investigations apart from his researches into scriptural exegesis (the scientific explication of biblical texts).

The results of this labour were published in a large monograph called, translating the original Dutch, *Jesus, the Story of the Living One* (or 'The Story of One Alive': *Jezus, het verhaal van een levende*, 1974). This work is the centre-piece of Schillebeeckx's entire theological output. It is a pathbreaking work for twentieth-century

Roman Catholic theology in that it constitutes the first really comprehensive probe on the part of a Catholic to examine Christian origins with the aid of a multitude of contemporary exegetical studies. Hans Küng published an interpretation of Christianity in non-metaphysical categories in the same year (see his *Christ sein*, 1974; Eng. trans. *On Being a Christian*, 1977), but it is not as avowedly exegetical as Schillebeeckx's book.

Jesus, the Story of the Living One was the first in a triptych of Christological studies. I shall not describe these three books here because I shall address the entire subject of Schillebeeckx's Christology in Chapter 6. Suffice it to remark at this stage that none of the English translations of the books' titles literally corresponds to the Dutch originals. In English, the first volume appeared as *Jesus: An Experiment in Christology* (1979). The second part of the English title is taken from an expression in the preface to the Dutch version. The second volume was produced with the title *Christ: The Christian Experience in the Modern World* (1980), whereas the Dutch has *Justice and Love: Grace and Liberation (Gerechtigheid en liefde: Genade en bevrijding*, 1977). And finally, the concluding part bears the title of *Church: The Human Story of God* (1990), while the original speaks of *Human Beings as God's Story (Mensen als verhaal van God*, 1989). The Dutch titles indicate two things very clearly. First, that narrative (*het verhaal*) has become a prominent aspect of Schillebeeckx's theology. And secondly, that, very obviously with the second volume, he acknowledges the political ramifications of Christian faith and sees his work as a Western form of a theology of liberation. Gustavo Gutiérrez (b. 1928) published his *Teología de la liberación* in 1971 (Eng. trans. *A Theology of Liberation*, 1973). His work is not mentioned in the first instalment of Schillebeeckx's Christological trilogy, but is discussed in the last two.

Moreover, while Schillebeeckx's articles of the 1940s and 1950s did not examine sensitive political problems bedevilling Flanders at the time, the second part of his later trilogy on Jesus and Christian identity is unmistakably attuned to the way political and economic exigencies impinge on Christian life. For example, alluding to what he calls the 'anti-communist instinct', he has this to say:

It is a fact that the churches with all their institutions are an integral part of bourgeois society, with which they are linked by countless threads. The sociological 'law of institutions' is particularly clear at this point. In given historical conditions these churches can only continue to exist, economically, if in fact they borrow from this bourgeois society. In that case they become assimilated to prevailing political and economic systems. In this situation the possibility for development in any church institution, even if it means to be utterly in accordance with the gospel, is specifically dependent on the potentialities of late capitalism and is tied to those possibilities. That is a fact which is documented by the contributions made by capitalist sources towards so-called 'non-progressive' activities in the churches. The consequence of this situation is that it prevents these churches from speaking a liberating word at a time of crisis. Even if churches inwardly dissociate themselves from a system which makes the rich richer and the poor poorer, institutionally they are so tied up with the system that they have to keep their mouths shut. In order to be able to present their message, they have to keep quiet about this message! That is the vicious circle in this situation. In order to be able to continue to exist as a church, people keep silent about the demands of the gospel. Can the churches have forgotten that following Jesus can also cost them their lives? (II, pp. 788–9)

THE CHURCH

In the preface to Schillebeeckx's third Christological volume he observes that in a period of ecclesiastical malaise and polarization it is better for a theologian to explore the heart of the Christian religion and the gospel than to become directly concerned with domestic, and hence secondary, church problems. And yet during the late 1970s, and throughout the 1980s, that is precisely what he did. Rather than proceeding to complete his Christological trilogy soon after the publication of the second part in 1977, he began to analyse the theology and practice of ministry. The third volume, as we have recorded, did not appear until 1989. In the interim, he became involved in Dutch conflicts relating to ministry and ecclesiastical government. After Vatican II the formation of a Dutch National Pastoral Council was announced in the Netherlands in 1966. One of its purposes was to involve people in ecclesiastical leadership who were neither bishops, presbyters, nor deacons. It effectively attempted to develop a more collegial or democratic form of church leadership, rather than to maintain a hierarchical pattern of government. It met between 1966 and 1970.

During the 1970s there were several exchanges and arguments between Dutch bishops and theologians on the one hand, and theologians involved with directing the affairs of the Vatican's administration on the other. In any event, the initiatives of the National Pastoral Council were not squashed once it dispersed, and interest gestated throughout the Netherlands to form small communities of Christians interested in new forms of ministry, politically aware, and concerned to combat the justification of injustice. In response to the demands of critically engaged communities of Christians, Schillebeeckx embarked on an inquiry into forms of Christian ministry and the nature of the Church. In a certain sense, however, his pastoral responsiveness to crises triggered by disputes over ecclesiastical organization in the Dutch Roman Catholic Church was somewhat regrettable, not because it assisted particular groups within the Dutch Catholic Church, but because it considerably delayed the completion of his Christological trilogy.

That said, Schillebeeckx's writings over the past two decades do record noteworthy conclusions concerning the Church and its ministry. Even though the third part of the Christological trilogy is not an ecclesiology or an avowedly explicit tract on the nature of the Church, its fourth chapter is taken up by an examination of different ways in which the church is and was understood. Not insignificantly, the chapter bears the title 'Towards democratic rule of the Church as a community of God'. According to Schillebeeckx, the *radical* difference which Vatican II brought about in the life of Catholics is that it rejected a Neoplatonic–hierarchical conception of the Church in favour of a Church wherein all believers should be able to participate in decisions relating to the Church's government (III, pp. 206 and 209). Schillebeeckx now points out, rightly in my opinion, and however daring it might appear on first hearing, that there is no place for a hierarchy in the Church. While the Church requires authoritative leadership, the functioning of a hierarchy is an extra-biblical importation into the life of the Church. Schillebeeckx argues that the idea of a church hierarchy conceived as a pyramidal structure of the Church, with Pope and bishops at the summit of the pyramid, is a structure extrapolated from the *imperium* of Graeco-Roman times and fortified by the Neoplatonic writings of Pseudo-Dionysius (fifth century), who tried to reinforce the notion of hierarchy philosophically (III, pp. 216–17). On a theological plane, Schillebeeckx commends the view that pyramidal hierarchy has been bolstered ideologically on the basis of a deficient Christology and an exaggerated estimation of the Pope's function in the Catholic Church. The Christological deficiency resides in a view that restricts the influence of the Holy Spirit of Christ to Church leaders (hierarchs) and forgets that the Spirit blows, as it were, among all believers. Furthermore, an inflated mysticism of papal infallibility coupled with a papal personality cult overlooks, as far as Schillebeeckx is concerned, the fact that the papal office is merely one among many ministries in the Church (see III, pp. 198–9).

There is quite a precise personal history behind the way Schillebeeckx now speaks about his Church. Just before Vatican II began, during which he was present as adviser to the Dutch primate, he helped to compose a pastoral letter for the Dutch bishops that was distributed among Dutch Catholics to prepare them for the Council. I referred to the text above. The letter spoke about the idea of collegiality, or shared responsibility among bishops in the direction of the Church. Vatican II met in four sessions spread over as many years. After the first session in 1962, Schillebeeckx wrote an article commenting on the session's evolution. Presciently, he had this to say:

> Completely unresolved still is the problem of the relationship between the 'collegiate' government of the Church (by the world episcopacy under the leadership of the Pope) and the 'central' government of the ecclesiastical Curia. I think that this problem

is going to be the main issue of the second phase of this council, if God grants John XXIII time to bring *his* Council to an end.[16]

John died the following year, leaving the way for Paul VI to preside over subsequent conciliar assemblies. During the third and fourth sessions of the Council the idea of collegiality was hotly contested, though finally accepted. And yet, portentously for Schillebeeckx, in November of 1964, Pope Paul appended an explanatory note, called a *nota explicativa* or *nota praevia*, to the Constitution (*Lumen Gentium*) being prepared by the bishops on the nature of the Church. The note effectively insisted that the Pope could, in given circumstances, rule the Church in his own right without wider consultation among bishops. I commented a short while ago that there is a personal history behind the way Schillebeeckx now speaks about the Church because, observing Paul's intervention with the *nota praevia*, he became extremely unsettled by what he regarded as a minority theological opinion overturning or severely curtailing the majority view of the bishops who had affirmed collegiality. The Constitution on the Church was approved in the final session of the Council with Pope Paul's note still included. Schillebeeckx later called the week following the last session as the Council's 'black week' (GNM, p. 122). He currently describes the period after the Council as 'the time of the anti-council' (FSG, p. 136): 'For the moment the "spirit of Vatican II" is indeed dead and gone in the official Roman Catholic church' (FSG. p. 139).

Note well the assertion that Vatican II's spirit is dead in the *official* Church. Schillebeeckx is convinced that what Vatican II intended to reform in the life of the Roman Catholic Church is now continued in grass roots, unofficial, ecclesiastical communities in the Netherlands and elsewhere (FSG, p. 139). Once he perceived what he regarded as an officially sanctioned attempt at the highest level of government in the Church to dampen the Council's idea of collegiality, he was faced with the quite pressing and personal question of how to go forward in his Church: 'after the Second Vatican Council and especially when the reactionary forces in the Church paralyzed all progress—that was from about 1969 or 1970 onwards—it became not just a theological question for me, but a really existential question: How should I proceed?' (GNM, p. 82). He proceeded by aligning himself with small, critical communities that he witnessed sprouting throughout the Church. In these he saw the Church's future. Indeed, as he surmises, 'the future of all religions will be found less in the great, "official" religious institutions than in the smaller, vital basic communities, living centres in which both mysticism and prophecy can be heard and seen' (GAU, pp. 173–4).

Responding to Vatican II's endorsement of the notion of a universal Church, Schillebeeckx insists in his publications on ministry that the universal Church is present in particular, local churches. Once more, we come across his all-important interest in the interchange between universality and particularity. Of special note with regard to his discussions of the universality of the Church is that he takes issue with Karl Rahner's view. As Schillebeeckx would have it, Rahner wrongly perceives the universal Church in the college of bishops who are said to constitute a supra-regional personnel in the Church. *Pace* Rahner, Schillebeeckx attests that such a view has no basis either in the factual history of the Church or in the documents of Vatican II. Rather, people who belong to local communities are the ones who constitute the universal Church. Otherwise put, people belong to the universal Church because they belong to a particular community (Min, p. 73).

At the heart of Schillebeeckx's understanding of the Church as the community of God wherein all members share responsibility is, not simply a personal history, but a firm view of what the Christian gospel entails. For Schillebeeckx, that gospel is very much encapsulated in the New Testament narratives, like Luke 22: 24–27, which forbid Christians to exercise lordship over others and among themselves. The gospel, then, is a proclamation of justice for those excommunicated by the lords of societies. It impels believers to establish community and communication with all those who have been excluded from society's embrace (see GNM, p. 79; and GAU, pp. 180–7). In Schillebeeckx's eyes, however, the Church has developed in such a way historically 'that it has in fact become a power over and against the gospel' (GNM, p. 80).

In sum, it seems clear that Schillebeeckx was greatly taken by Vatican II's insistence that all believers have the right and duty to be responsible for the Church's task of proclaiming the gospel of justice. His work among critical grass roots communities in the Netherlands is impelled by a marked dissatisfaction that the promise of a Council of bishops — Vatican II — to reform the Church under the pretext of collegiality was not eventually encoded in ecclesiastical law. Subsequently, Vatican II's radical change from a hierarchically to a collegially conceived Church, and its recognition of believers' rights to act freely in ecclesiastical tasks, were not given either institutional or legal protection (see III, p. 207):

> And when this Christian freedom recognized by the council was not subsequently guaranteed and protected by church law, this promise became an empty gesture, without any evangelical influence in our history. Then the breath of the council was cut off and its spirit, the Holy Spirit, was extinguished. Then, by virtue of various concerns (which were often matters of church politics), church hierarchies achieved an uncontrolled power over men and women of God, 'God's people on the way', who had been put under tutelage. (III, p. xiv)

We need not allow ourselves to go so far as to say that Vatican II's spirit, reportedly the Holy Spirit, has been extinguished in the wake of the Council, but we do catch a glimpse with this text of just how deeply felt Schillebeeckx's recent writings on the Church are. They are so deeply felt, in fact, and are so coloured by his experiences in the Netherlands, that one would do well to weigh his judgements with care. For example, on what basis apart from his Dutch experiences does he find cause to draw the rather inflated conclusion that 'never before have women and men, the so-called laity, been so committed to the work of the local church for the church and the world as a whole' (ibid.)?

MINISTRY

Throughout his career Schillebeeckx has frequently had occasion to publish articles relating to the theology and practice of ministry in the Church. In the late 1970s, however, and throughout the 1980s, his time became increasingly absorbed by the task of rethinking the nature and function of ministry, especially within the Roman Catholic Church.

In 1979, Nijmegen's faculty of theology conducted a seminar on the whole matter of ministry, and probed especially the questions as to whether women and married people could be ordained to official ministries. Schillebeeckx produced a paper for the seminar that was subsequently published in *Tijdschrift voor Theologie*. It appeared in English in 1980, along with contributions from other academics, in the book *Minister? Pastor? Prophet?: Grass Roots Leadership in the Churches*.[17] Schillebeeckx's contribution was called 'A creative retrospect as inspiration for the ministry in the future' (pp. 57–84). As the title suggests, the article scans Christian history to uncover theological and historical principles which might point a direction for new forms of ministry in the future. The main lines of argument deployed in the text found their way into two subsequent books by Schillebeeckx on ministry. Once again, the titles of the English translations of the books do not correspond exactly to the Dutch originals. The first appeared in 1980 as, to render the Dutch, *Church Ministry: Leaders in the Community of Jesus Christ*. It was issued in English in 1981 as *Ministry: A Case for Change*, and followed in 1985 with a more amplified treatment in a book called, translating the Dutch, *A Defence for People in the Church: Christian Identity and Ministries in the Church*. In English, it bore the title *The Church with a Human Face: A New and Expanded Theology of Ministry*.[18]

The theology of ministry enunciated in the article and two subsequent books generated extensive discussion and criticism in the Netherlands and beyond. One scholar, Pierre Grelot, even went to the trouble of writing a book to refute aspects of Schillebeeckx's conclusions.[19] However, in the same year as Grelot published his book, Yves Congar (b. 1904) welcomed Schillebeeckx's second book on ministry with the French drinking salute: *Santé*.[20] Of the same work, a professor in the University of Edinburgh, James P. Mackey, said that it 'should be required reading for all educated Catholics'.[21] Elsewhere, Mackey opines that 'Schillebeeckx in his later years has proved to be the true pioneer of contemporary Roman Catholic theology'.[22]

That may or may not be the case, but in any event, Schillebeeckx conceded himself that his first book on ministry was faulty in some of its historical conclusions (see CHF, p. 124). A major difference between the two books is that the second is prefaced by a brief Christological exposition (pp. 13–39), in the light of which Schillebeeckx's conclusions concerning ministry are made. For anyone looking for a condensed expression of his Christology, these pages make fruitful reading.

But what, in a nutshell, was the upshot of Schillebeeckx's researches into the history and practice of ministry? I shall gather together here, for the purposes of stark summary, some of the major points in the article on ministry that was published in English in 1980.

In the first place, Schillebeeckx concludes that ministry is a function for a community and not a status (see p. 61). Second, he draws attention to what he regards as quite a fundamental alteration that transpired in attitudes to ministry with the Third and Fourth Lateran Councils, held respectively in 1179 and 1215 (p. 65). For Schillebeeckx, with respect to ministry, the Third Lateran Council effectively divides the first Christian millennium from the second (p. 66), and broke with a tradition stemming from the Council of Chalcedon (451). For the latter, someone who has been chosen by a *particular* community may be ordained to ministry (p. 58). The former weakened the claim of a community to be able to choose its ministerial leader, and the theological view subsequently developed was sanctioned by the Council of Trent in the sixteenth century, according to which one could be ordained in an 'absolute' sense, that is, independently of the choice of a particular community (see p. 66). We can see now where this line of argument is leading Schillebeeckx: 'the earlier ecclesial view of the ministry should have priority over the conception which has been regarded as official since then' (p. 67). In other words, what was possible formerly should be possible latterly.

With regard to the priesthood, Schillebeeckx distinguishes three different understandings of it: patristic, feudal, and modern. He concludes that it was only in modern times, after the sixteenth century, that a completely clerical and hierarchical view of priesthood developed and held sway right up until Vatican II (pp. 71–2).

Much more could be said to do justice to Schillebeeckx's arguments concerning ministry, but lack of space prohibits. Suffice it to emphasize that his entire discussion of both the Church and its ministries unfolds in association with his conviction that the Church does not exist to serve itself. Nor is it the kingdom of God. It anticipates that kingdom when it joins the world, so to speak, to bring about justice where injustice prevails.[23]

SERMONS AND OCCASIONAL ADDRESSES

So much for matters of Church and ministry. In addition to scholarly or popular essays, Schillebeeckx has also outlined his theology in the setting of worship or liturgy. In the 1980s he published two collections of his sermons, or homilies, as well as occasional speeches. We have previously had occasion to refer to these books. The first was called *Evangelie verhalen* (1982; Eng. trans. *God Among Us: The Gospel Proclaimed,* 1983). The second appeared in 1988 with the title *Om het behoud van het evangelie: Evangelie verhalen*, deel II (Eng. trans. *For the Sake of the Gospel*, 1989). Both volumes contain quite pithy statements of the essential themes of Schillebeeckx's theology, and presage material that eventually appeared in the third part of his Christological trilogy.

IS POLITICS EVERYTHING?

In 1986 Schillebeeckx released a small book containing a series of lectures, the Abraham Kuyper Lectures, he gave in the Free University of Amsterdam in the same year. One could be forgiven for failing to appreciate what is involved in the book's original Dutch title: *If Politics Is Not Everything . . . Jesus in Western Culture*. The book appeared in a British edition as *Jesus in Our Western Culture: Mysticism, Ethics and Politics*; and in a North American form as *On Christian Faith: The Spiritual, Ethical, and Political Dimensions*.[24] The original Dutch text responds to the title and content of another book, by a professor of the Free University of Amsterdam. The work in question is Harry M. Kuitert's treatise *Everything Is Politics but Politics Is Not Everything: A Theological Perspective on Faith and Politics*. It was published in Dutch in 1985 and argues, among other things, that although the political side to faith and the Church was justifiably recognized in the 1960s, too much has been made of it in theological discussions: politics has taken hold of church preaching, discussion, and theology.[25] What needs to be noted about Schillebeeckx's response to Kuitert is that the former commends the view that, when speaking about the political dimension of faith, one should not reduce politics to the mere matter of government. On the contrary, and more expansively understood, the term politics denotes 'an intensive form of social commitment (and thus not the political activity of professional politicians *per se*), a commitment accessible to all people' (JWC, p. 72).

In subsequent chapters I shall refer to this book frequently. It is relatively short and contains a concise summary of Schillebeeckx's mature theological reflection. The four chapters of the text explore his pivotal interests:

> In these lectures I want to talk about God—about God in his or her relation to men and women and therefore about the mystical or theologal, the ethical and the political dimension of this belief in God, all viewed from the focal point of Jesus of Nazareth, whom the church confesses as the Christ. (JWC, p. vii)

As always, Schillebeeckx attends to the two pillars of Christian faith — God and Christ — and he speaks about the latter to elucidate the meaning of faith in the former. And once more, in addition, he seeks to elaborate how human beings can be said to stand in relation to God. When speaking about human encounters with God, Schillebeeckx uses the word 'theologal', which is a neologism in both Dutch and English. As a technical theological term it is a close equivalent to the word 'supernatural'. Schillebeeckx prefers to speak of a theologal relationship with God, it would seem, or of the theologal dimension of faith, because the term 'supernatural' simply refers to that which is beyond nature and does not necessarily imply a reciprocity between nature and supernature. The word 'theologal', on the other hand, functions in Schillebeeckx's theology to designate a dynamic interrelationship between God and people which attends to faith.

CONCLUSION

My overview of Schillebeeckx's more significant works and their themes has been necessarily quite selective. Nonetheless, in ensuing chapters I shall refer to some of his other works so as to amplify points made above. By surveying his more consequential publications and prominent themes, it becomes evident that throughout his career he has remained stalwartly convinced that Christian faith in a Creator God, who offers salvation through creation and in the figure of Jesus of Nazareth, is a faith which actually augments human freedom. In a post-Enlightenment European setting, Schillebeeckx's theological output indeed takes issue with the notion that Christian faith is atavistic and enslaved to outworn ideas of yesteryear.

And it is in this light that another, hitherto unaccentuated theme requires to be emphasized. Running throughout Schillebeeckx's writings is a motif of hope. During his retirement speech at Nijmegen's university, he declared that he regarded his speech as his 'theological testament'. He concluded his address by quoting a verse from St Paul which speaks of the grieving of those bereft of hope (1 Thessalonians 4: 13). Schillebeeckx's works attempt to inculcate hope in those unsettled by baleful histories of suffering, those in circumstances of cultural travail and change, and where Christianity is stigmatized as a suppression of freedom. In his own words:

> precisely in this Western social climate of secularization and religious indifference, of the spread of science, technology and instrumental thinking in terms of means to an end, the question of God becomes the freest and most gratuitous question that one can ask, and the way to God also becomes the freest career to choose.[26]

Notes

1 GAU, p. 124. In addition, see III, p. 15.
2 On the significance of Kant's theory of knowledge, and of his importance for modern theology, see, respectively, John Hick, *An Interpretation of Religion: Human Responses to the Transcendent* (Basingstoke: Macmillan, 1989), pp. 240-1; and Kenneth Surin, *The Turnings of Darkness and Light: Essays in Philosophical and Systematic Theology* (Cambridge: Cambridge University Press, 1989), p. 273, n. 19.
3 See GNM, p. 112; GAU, p. 214; and III, pp. 53 (on the French Revolution), 200 and 222.
4 Schillebeeckx's acknowledgement that he stands in two positive traditions, those of the Enlightenment and Christianity, is contained in an exchange between himself and Leo Apostel. See Edward Schillebeeckx and Leo Apostel, 'Godgelovigheid en vrijzinnigheid bevraagd', *Tijdschrift voor Geestelijk Leven,* extra number: *(A)theïstische Spiritualiteit* (1988), pp. 7-28 (p. 9).
5 For Aquinas's statement of the principle see his *Summa Theologiae*, II-II, q. 1, a. 2, ad 2. For an illustration of Schillebeeckx's subsequent reliance on Aquinas's maxim see the former's GFM, pp. 3, 13, and 42; as well as III, chs 1 and 2, esp. pp. 33-45 and 74-7.
6 I, p. 30. For an important study of Schillebeeckx's work in a soteriological vein, see Tadahiko Iwashima, *Menschheitsgeschichte und Heilserfahrung: Die Theologie von Edward Schillebeeckx als methodisch reflektierte Soteriologie* (Düsseldorf: Patmos, 1982).
7 The full title is *De Sacramentele Heilseconomie: Theologische bezinning op S. Thomas' sacramentenleer in het licht van de traditie en van de hedendaagse sacramentproblematiek* (Antwerp/Bilthoven: H. Nelissen, 1952).
8 See Edward Schillebeeckx, *De Christusontmoeting als sacrament van de Godsontmoeting* (Antwerp/Bilthoven: H. Nelissen, 1958); and *Christus sacrament van de Godsontmoeting* (Bilthoven: H. Nelissen, 1959), of which CS is the English translation.
9 Consult Edward Schillebeeckx, 'Maria' in H. Brink et al. (eds), *Theologisch Woordenboek*, 3 vols (Roermond and Masseik: J. J. Roman and Zonen, 1952-8), II (1957), cols 3078-3151; *Maria, Christus' mooiste wonderschepping* (Antwerp: Apostolaat van de Rosenkrans, 1954); and *Maria, moeder van de verlossing* (Antwerp/Haarlem: Apostolaat van de Rosenkrans, 1955), of which M is the English translation.
10 Pierre Gisel, *Vérité et Histoire* (Paris: Editions Beauchesne, 1977).
11 For confirmation of the comments made on the two lectures, see Edward Schillebeeckx, *Op zoek naar de levende God* (Utrecht and Nijmegen: Dekker and Van de Vegt, 1958), which is partly reproduced in GM, ch. 2; and *Theologisch Geloofsverstaan Anno 1983* (Baarn: H. Nelissen, 1983), part of which is rehearsed in III, pp. 40-5.
12 FSG, p. 167. For Schillebeeckx's original work on marriage see *Het huwelijk: aardse werkelijkheid en heilsmysterie* (Bilthoven: H. Nelissen, 1963). The English translation is: *Marriage: Human Reality and Saving Mystery* (London: Sheed & Ward, 1965/1984).
13 Edward Schillebeeckx, *Clerical Celibacy Under Fire: A Critical Appraisal* (London and Sydney: Sheed & Ward, 1968), pp. 1-2. The Dutch original is *Het ambts-celibaat in de branding: een kritische bezinning* (Bilthoven: H. Nelissen, 1966). For Schillebeeckx's interpretation of Vatican II's achievement, see his book *Vatican II: The Real Achievement* (London and Melbourne: Sheed & Ward, 1967).
14 There is no Dutch version of GFM. The Dutch edition of *The Eucharist*

(London: Sheed & Ward, 1968) is to be found in Schillebeeckx's *Christus' tegenwoordigheid in de eucharistie* (Bilthoven: H. Nelissen, 1967).

15 All of the Dutch originals were published in the Netherlands by H. Nelissen. English translations of each volume were published by Sheed & Ward in London in, successively, 1967, 1969, 1971, 1973, and 1974.

16 Edward Schillebeeckx, 'Vatican II: impressions of a struggle of minds', *Life of the Spirit* 17 (1963), pp. 499–505 (pp. 504–5).

17 Lucas Grollenberg, Jan Kerkhofs, Anton Houtepen, J. J. A. Volleberg and Edward Schillebeeckx, *Minister? Pastor? Prophet?: Grass Roots Leadership in the Churches* (London: SCM, 1980).

18 For the content of the four books just mentioned see Edward Schillebeeckx, *Kerkelijk ambt: Voorgangers in de gemeente van Jezus Christus* (Bloemendaal: H. Nelissen,1980); Min; *Pleidooi voor mensen in de kerk: Christelijke identiteit en ambten in de kerk* (Baarn: H. Nelissen, 1985); and CHF.

19 Pierre Grelot, *Les ministères dans le people de Dieu* (Paris: Du Cerf, 1988).

20 Yves Congar, 'Bulletin d'Ecclésiologie', *Revue des Sciences Philosophiques et Théologiques* 72 (1988), pp. 109–19 (p. 114).

21 In James D. G. Dunn and James P. Mackey, *New Testament Theology in Dialogue: Christology and Ministry* (Philadelphia: The Westminster Press, 1987), p. 119, n. 3.

22 James P. Mackey, *Modern Theology: A Sense of Direction* (Oxford: Oxford University Press, 1987), p. 142.

23 See Edward Schillebeeckx, 'Christian conscience and nuclear deterrent', *Doctrine and Life* 32 (1982), pp. 98–122 (pp. 102–12); and III, ch. 5.

24 See Edward Schillebeeckx, *Als politiek niet alles is: Jezus in de westerse cultuur: Abraham Kuyper-lezingen 1986* (Baarn: Ten Have, 1986). The British edn: London: SCM, 1987; and the North American: New York: Crossroad, 1987.

25 See H. M. Kuitert, *Alles is politiek maar politiek is niet alles: een theologisch perspectief op geloof en politiek* (Baarn: Ten Have, 1985), p. 9. John Bowden has translated the book as *Everything Is Politics but Politics Is Not Everything: A Theological Perspective on Faith and Politics* (London: SCM/Grand Rapids: Eerdmans, 1986).

26 JWC, p. 5. For the conclusion of Schillebeeckx's retirement speech, see his *Theologische Geloofsverstaan Anno 1983*, p. 21.

5

'I believe in God, Creator of heaven and earth'

The stated aim of this book is not to provide an exhaustive and detailed exposition of Edward Schillebeeckx's theology, which is in any case impossible since he continues to develop and publish his ideas. Instead, its purpose is to explain why he may be regarded as an outstanding Christian thinker; to provide an interpretation of the essential features of his theology; and, for the interested inquirer, to furnish a ready access to the core of his theology as it is currently in hand. The following chapter explains that core in connection with the notion of creation.[1]

Schillebeeckx uses a variety of expressions to speak of God. He refers to God, for instance, as: 'a familiar friend'; 'the one who was and is to come'; an 'absolute freedom', who is 'eternally young', 'new each moment', 'a constant surprise', 'concerned for humankind', 'more human than any human being', and 'the source of pure positivity'.[2] All of these expressions stem from a more fundamental and classically Christian understanding of God as creator (*Deus Creator*): '. . . God is essentially creator, the lover of ·he finite, loving with the absoluteness of a divine love which is unfathomable to us' (III, p. 181). In 1968 Schillebeeckx observed that 'the dogma of creation and the metaphysical realism that is the consequence of this dogma are at the centre of all theological speculation'.[3] The metaphysical realism spoken of here asserts that there is a reality external to the human mind, and that extra-mental reality is not a product of the mind. In 1989 Schillebeeckx propounded that belief in creation is perhaps for Christians 'not the focus of their belief, but the background and horizon of all Christian belief' (III, p. 90). Again and again in his publications he relies on a particular understanding of creation to explain the nature and distinctiveness of Christian faith.[4]

One of my major conclusions with respect to the task of interpreting the essential features and core of Schillebeeckx's theology is that, in order for his work to be properly understood, it is necessary to search for the philosophical arguments that underlie his theological statements. Ever since he was a young man he has been a fervid reader of philosophy. In this light, it is advisable to consider what kind of philosophical position sustains his discourses on Christian faith in creation if his discourses are to be suitably comprehended.

THE EXPERIENCE OF FINITUDE

The philosophical expression of the idea that Christian faith annuls human freedom is not the only position with which Schillebeeckx's theology takes issue. He also forswears the proposition that finitude is the only reality there is. Particularly since the seventeenth century, what could be called a philosophy of immanence or finitude made its presence felt in the writings of some prominent Western European philosophers. Endorsed thematically in the works of Baruch Spinoza, it resurfaces in the publications of Kant, Hegel, Marx, Freud and Sartre, to name but a few. The philosophy or idea I am alluding to can be stated baldly in this way: finite, limited, historical human existence is the only existence which prevails, for there are neither supernatural potencies, nor values, nor a personal Creator-God existing apart from and beyond the worldly, profane existence in which human beings find themselves. The notion that finitude or immanence is the sum total of existence is certainly not new and found ancient enunciations in Pre-Socratic, Epicurean and Stoic philosophies. A contemporary British thinker espouses essentially the same idea by observing that 'our knowledge-systems, our beliefs, our myths, our norms, our meanings, even our values, are as human and local and transient as we are. *That* is the thought that freezes the blood.'[5] It is worth noting in passing, that the aforementioned philosophy of immanence, according to which finitude is all-that-is, is closely related to the ideas of freedom and emancipation: to perceive that everything which exists is finite, is, so the argument suggests, to emancipate oneself from tutelage to non-existent deities and values.

Schillebeeckx's creation-based theology is rooted in a notion of finitude. Explained in the plainest of terms, to speak of finitude, contingency, or immanence, is simply to refer to human beings' experiences of their limitations and mortality. For humans are neither lords nor masters of either themselves or the universe, and they do not find within themselves either the necessary reason for, or the absolute cause of, their existence (see III, p. 78).

As a young man, Schillebeeckx read many philosophical treatments of immanence. But when he studied in France between 1946 and 1947, he encountered in a book by Sartre a particularly acute philosophical analysis and robust acknowledgement of finitude, or this-worldliness. While in Paris, he undertook a close reading of Sartre's tract *L'être et le néant* (Eng. trans. *Being and Nothing-*

ness), under the supervision of Louis Lavelle. The tract had been published in Paris during 1943, just a few years before his arrival there. Over forty years after reading Sartre, Schillebeeckx was able to observe: 'No one has analysed this radical finitude of being human in this contingent world better than an agnostic who was originally in fact a militant atheist, Jean-Paul Sartre' (III, p. 78). An important upshot of Schillebeeckx's attention to Sartre's analysis of contingency is his confirmation of the latter's conclusion that human existence is essentially and radically finite. Furthermore, Schillebeeckx advances the conclusion that believers and non-believers alike share a pre-linguistic experience of being utterly constrained by finitude.

Now the point to bear in mind at all costs at this juncture is that Schillebeeckx, unlike agnostic or atheistic philosophers of immanence who toll the knell of Christianity, actually regards an experience of finitude as the very source of belief in God as creator, and not as an indication that God is non-existent. For Schillebeeckx, all human beings undergo pre-linguistic experiences of radical limitation, or finitude, in situations where they feel most vulnerable — situations, for example, which are marked by sickness, death or plagues. He commends the perspective that although both believers and non-believers have similar experiences of finitude, they nonetheless interpret them in different ways. For the non-believer, finitude is the amplitude and parameter of human existence, so to speak. For the believer, the human experience of being finite and contingent can be interpreted as a pointer to God. For Schillebeeckx, finitude is another term for secularity and can be construed as a reference to the source of secularity, namely, a divine creator:

> for the believer, non-divine finitude is precisely the place where the infinite and the finite come most closely into contact. From this close contact of the secular and the transcendent, the infinite and the finite, there arises, as mystics say, the spark of the soul; there all religion takes fire.[6]

WORKS DEALING WITH CREATION

In Chapter 1 I commented on a number of factors which render Schillebeeckx's theology somewhat difficult to unravel. Here I mention yet another: Schillebeeckx is a systematic theologian who has never produced a systematic theology. He is a dogmatician without a dogmatics. In other words, he has never attempted to produce a sweeping and systematically ordered presentation of Christian faith in the manner, let us say, of Karl Barth (1886–1968), Hendrikus Berkhof (b. 1914), or Wolfhart Pannenberg. Nevertheless, while he has not published a self-styled, all-encompassing systematic theology, when he returned to Louvain after his sojourn in France, he did compose quite thoroughgoing treatments of major theological themes such as creation and Christology. Upon his return in 1947, he immediately set about teaching dogmatic theology in the Dominican House of Studies. During the academic year of 1956–57, which is to say, towards the end of his tenure in Louvain, he distributed among his students a two-volume manuscript of his lecture material on creation entitled *Theologische Bezinning op het Scheppingsgeloof* ('The Theological Consciousness of Creation-Faith').[7] I shall subsequently refer to this work as *Creation*. This typed manuscript of seven hundred pages is not merely a vast quarry of interpretations of Christian belief in creation in which Schillebeeckx explains creation-faith with reference to the French atheistic existentialism that he scrutinized in Paris (see vol. II, pp. 262–71). It is also is a highly useful aid to understanding his entire theological project, because his later and even most recent publications are replete with explanations and concepts about God that were first elaborated in these lectures. A comparison between the lectures and later publications supports the conclusion that the topic of creation has been pivotal in Schillebeeckx's theology throughout his career. To drive the point home, his early and later theological expositions of creation are at base entirely homologous, even though his latest works are more concerned with ecological matters.

Apart from brief and recurrent references to creation in Schillebeeckx's works, and in addition to the Louvain lecture material, there are three singularly succinct expositions of creation-faith contained in his books *God Among Us*, *Interim Report on the Books 'Jesus' and 'Christ'*, and *Church: The Human Story of God*.[8] My exposition of his understanding of creation in ensuing pages relies mainly on these three books and on the lecture material, *Creation*. Each of these four sources follows exactly the same line of argument.

I shall preface my exposition by alluding to difficulties commonly associated with the Christian doctrine of creation. Then I turn to a consideration of what Schillebeeckx regards as misunderstandings of faith in creation. This consideration sets the stage for an examination of how creation is to be more adequately understood in a theological fashion. A further section pays attention to the problem of evil, or, as some would prefer, the enigma of suffering in a world that is supposed to have issued from an all-powerful and all-loving God.

DIFFICULTIES WITH THE DOCTRINE OF CREATION

The idea of a divine creation is the first to be professed in time-honoured Christian creeds: 'I believe in God, Creator of heaven and earth'. It is also one of the first to be jettisoned in a supposed post-Enlightenment intellectual war between religion and science, where the latter is thought to have overthrown the former as an authoritative source for explaining the nature of the world. Stated otherwise, and to generalize broadly, creation is a belief commonly thought to have been overturned by modern empirical sciences that have developed since the European Renaissance. In the sixteenth century, voyages of discovery charted the 'New World' and thereby challenged both biblical and mediaeval cosmographical representations of our planet. Coupled with geographical discoveries came new astronomical and physical explanations of material reality, represented in works such as Nicolas Copernicus's (1473–1543) *De revolutionibus orbium coelestium* (1543) and Isaac Newton's (1642–1727) *Philosophiae naturalis principia mathematica* (1687). In the last century, Charles Darwin's (1809–82) evolutionary speculations triggered a further questioning of the truth of the biblical picture of creation. Indeed, Jewish, Islamic and Christian views of creation easily appear to have little in common with specific contemporary scientific theories concerning the genesis and sustenance of the world. And so, confronted with cosmological hypotheses such as the Big-Bang and Steady-State theories, and quantum fluctuation, Christian theology can ask of itself: Is it really possible today to defend the first chapter of Genesis and the idea that God gave form to, and breathed life into, a primaeval chaos? One of the strengths of Schillebeeckx's theology rests in his ability to show that to reject the theological doctrine of creation on the grounds that it is incompatible with modern science is not only to misunderstand entirely what creation means theologically, but also to adhere to a redundant mechanistic understanding of physics. Moreover, his understanding of creation enables him to adopt a positive and optimistic stance with regard to human, secular, and this-worldly existence.

MISUNDERSTANDINGS OF CREATION

The distinctive features of Schillebeeckx's theology of creation can be seen more clearly when placed against the background of his discussions of misunderstandings of creation-faith. There are basically two sets of problems involved with the views of creation which he finds wanting. The first revolves around the notion of finitude. He labels three views as 'unchristian' to the extent that each of them, in different ways, fails to regard finitude in a positive light. To these three stances he gives the names dualism, emanationism and pantheism. Each regards finitude as a blemish. Another set of difficulties is to be found in viewpoints that regard creation solely as a physical explanation of the universe or as a chronological event. Let us turn, then, to a consideration of these misconceptions.

(a) Dualism

Schillebeeckx makes two principal observations when he speaks of a dualistic conception of creation.[9] First, he remarks that dualism arose from a sense of scandal and offence caused by the suffering, evil, injustice and meaninglessness encountered in our world, in nature, and throughout human history. He describes dualism as the denial that God willingly created the world and human beings *as they are*.

Dualism, therefore, regards finitude as an aberration and as an abnormal condition. It considers finitude as either the regrettable result of a fault in creation or the fruit of a primal sin. A view like this is called dualistic because it posits two powers that stand in need of compromise: on the one hand, the reality of God; and on the other, an inimical 'power of darkness'. Within a dualistic notion of creation, salvation is to be found either in a lost paradise situated in the past, or in an imagined apocalyptic new earth and new humanity yet to be inaugurated.

(b) Emanationism

Another way of misconstruing creation is represented by the idea that it is basically not worthy of God's involvement. This view, labelled emanationism, is not altogether unlike dualism in that it devalues finitude. It differs from dualism in that it does not arise from a sense of scandal at the demonstrable awfulness of much human existence, but from a willingness to emphasize the transcendence of God. By seeking to preserve God's transcendence, that is, God's ineffable 'otherness', emanationism contends that God is so exalted and aloof that a divine involvement with creation would only compromise the magnitude of divinity. To get round this difficulty, emanationism envisages that God entrusts dealings with creation to a lieutenant of lesser importance — like Plato's Demiurge. Emanationism is so tagged because it regards human beings and the world as degraded emanations of God.

(c) Pantheism

Occasionally God's presence in the world is taken to mean that everything else apart from God is in some manner to be explained either as an allusion to God or as a constituent of the actual definition of God. Once again, when it comes to pantheism, the difficulty for Christian faith centres on the question of finitude. For pantheism, finitude is annulled: God subsumes everything. According to Christian faith, however, finitude is not removed by God, but taken up, so to speak, into God's presence. In short, for Christians, the world and human beings are within God's presence, though totally other than God.

(d) Creation as an explanation or event in time

As far as Schillebeeckx is concerned, creation is misunderstood once again if it is esteemed as an explication of the world and the universe. Contrariwise, Christian faith in creation furnishes neither macrophysical nor microphysical data concerning the material genesis of the universe. This assertion is potentially the most perplexing aspect of Schillebeeckx's explanation of creation because creational doctrines are frequently regarded precisely as accounts of how the universe came into being and what it is like. But in Schillebeeckx's eyes the Christian doctrine of creation does not primarily amount to a cosmology. It does not explain the material genesis of reality. It is mischaracterized if it is *only* and primarily conceived as an account of how things and events came into being. Assuredly, creation-faith does not provide any information about the internal constitution of human beings or their world. Providing that information is the province of science, not of theology.

The distinguishing feature of traditional Christian faith in creation is the belief that everything which exists in the universe came into being with the action of an Uncreated Being. Nowhere does Schillebeeckx deny this belief. What he does discountenance is the assumption that creation only refers to God's creative action in the past. He avers that creation is a continuing and dynamic occurrence rather than a chronological event set somewhere at the beginning of time:

> God did not first create a primordial atom or a primordial mist, from which the whole of the world later came into being from within by means of gradual development, without any further activity on the part of God the creator. (WC, p. 242)

St Augustine (354–430) made similar points several centuries previously in his large work *The City of God*, as did Thomas Aquinas in his *Summa Theologiae* (Ia, 44–49).

Were creation to be understood as an explanation of material phenomena in history and nature, then it would follow that any attempt to change the phenomena would be blasphemous by virtue of a disregard for a divinely predetermined and preconceived universe (see GAU, p. 94). In Schillebeeckx's own, somewhat playful words:

> Belief in creation does not claim to give an explanation of the origin of the world. If God is said to be the *explanation* of the fact that things and events are what they are, then any attempt to change these things and situations (for better or for worse) is in fact blasphemous, or, on the other hand, it turns human beings and our whole world into a puppet-show in which God alone holds the strings in his hands behind the screen: human history as a large-scale Muppet show! (III, pp. 229–30)

THE LANGUAGES OF FAITH AND SCIENCE

Having drawn attention to unsatisfactory accounts of creation, we may now examine in greater detail Schillebeeckx's own explanation of Christian faith in God's creation.

But first, it may be helpful to make a brief philosophical detour to consider a question of language. In his book *Jesus: An Experiment in Christology,* Schillebeeckx discusses the creative activity of God in our world, and in the process draws a distinction between secular scientific language and faith-language (pp. 628–30). The central point to be gleaned from his distinction is that the two kinds of language refer to one and the same reality. He elaborated upon the distinction in a lecture, noted above (see p. 12 note 4), that was given in England and published in 1981. The lecture asserts that reality is one and the selfsame, but as such it can be contemplated from different formal points of view, or understood on different levels. Subsequently, the language of faith and empirically descriptive scientific language have recourse to exactly the same reality and do not stand in need of dialectical reconciliation. In terms of semiotics (the study of [linguistic] signs), the two formal points of view are dissymmetrical isotopes that are related antinomically only for the mind.[10] Hence, while religious language describing creation can certainly be either figurative, poetic, or metaphorical, it refers *really* to the same reality specified by science. Moreover, for Schillebeeckx, science is no more purely objective than other forms of knowledge (see III, pp. 3 and 78). In this light, a supposed antipathy between religious and scientific discourses is exposed as a pseudo-problem.

The philosophical point highlighted here is of the utmost importance for a correct understanding of Schillebeeckx's notion of creation. Ultimately, his religious faith in creation does not need to be reconciled with scientific explanations of the cosmos because science and religion speak about the same reality, though from different formal points of view. To oppose faith-language and empirical discourse is to fall prey to the philosophical error of confusing the order of reality with the order of knowledge. Expressed somewhat differently, that which is real cannot be equated with a particular form of human reflection such as philosophy, theology, or physical and analytical sciences.

WHAT CREATION IS

In Schillebeeckx's terms, creation is to be understood above all as a reality that says something about God and God's relation to human beings and their world. The theological meaning of faith in creation turns on the way God's nature *manifests* itself. Thus, faith in creation is concerned not so much with a definition of God, but with God's manifestation in worldly reality.[11]

The hallmark of Schillebeeckx's explanation of religious belief in creation is a recognition of *the worth of limitation*. In other words, that which is limited and finite constitutes the very place in which God's being is exhibited. Jewish–Christian faith in creation accommodates a dissimilarity between God and everything that is limited or contingent. The vital point here is that limitation is not regarded as something to be escaped from: contingency and finitude are not flaws. On the contrary, the divinity of God is recognized *in* the awareness that contingency is not a wound, evil or apostasy, but rather an essential goodness. To say this is another way of propounding, with St Thomas, that God can only be approached indirectly by way of created things.

Whenever Schillebeeckx comes to the point of illustrating exactly what he means by creation he always makes the same double-edged assertion about a single, divine act of creation which involves two subjects — a Creator and creatures.[12] In the first place, he specifies that creation means that God brings into being something which is non-divine. Creation thus construed is an action of God that establishes all that is finite, human and worldly. In the second place, *exactly the same action*, which confirms and affirms the secularity of the world, also discloses the inherent being of God as non-secular, transcendent reality.[13] Even though the conception of a single act founding our existence and simultaneously maintaining God's transcendence is present in Schillebeeckx's most recent works, it actually draws on earlier publications by Dominic De Petter (see GM, p. 167). A concise formulation of this double-sided affirmation is to be found in Schillebeeckx's short book *Jesus in Our Western Culture*:

> Creation is an action of God which on the one hand unconditionally gives us our finite, non-divine character, destined for true humanity, and on the other hand at the same time establishes God in disinterested love as our God: our salvation and happiness, the supreme content of true and good humanity. God freely creates humanity for salvation and human happiness, but in this same action, in sovereign freedom, he seeks himself to be the deepest meaning, salvation and happiness of human life. (JWC, pp. 17–18)

CREATION AND SALVATION

It is important to note that in the statement just quoted Schillebeeckx links the doctrine of creation to the question of human salvation. As far as he is aware, God's creation is also the beginning of a history of salvation (and perdition). Exactly the same point was made in his Louvain lectures on creation. In sum, therefore, God the Creator (*Deus Creator*) is also God the Saviour (*Deus Salutaris*).[14] In this wise, the doctrines of creation and salvation shed mutual light on each other. As stated by Schillebeeckx, the driving question of human history, especially in present times, is the issue of salvation: Who or what saves human beings from everything which threatens them? His reply is that ultimately, only God saves; God saves as Creator, in and through creation.[15]

With regard to the issue of salvation, I should note at this point that the contemporary German theologian Johann Baptist Metz has been developing a political theology since the mid-1960s. While Schillebeeckx's later theology most certainly recognizes a political dimension of Christian faith, it does not equate theology primarily with political concerns, but with issues concerning salvation and creation. Hence, one may conclude that Schillebeeckx's theology is a soteriology (a *Heilstheologie*) which now *includes* a political theology.[16]

THE BOUNDARY BETWEEN GOD AND THE NON-GODLY

In contrast to dualistic, emanationistic, and pantheistic views of creation, Schillebeeckx is keen to show that salvation from God never consists in God saving people from their finitude. In contrasting a Christian view of creation-faith with non-Christian perspectives, Schillebeeckx illuminates two basic aspects of the Christian approach.

To begin with, he stresses the intrinsic merit of finitude. Contingency is not a flaw but the very ground in which a distinction between God and people can be made. In other words, finitude represents a boundary between God and non-godly creatures. When explaining what he means by finitude, Schillebeeckx does not rely on a more classical idea of 'creation out of nothing', even though he does not dismiss the idea. He regards the formula of 'creation out of nothing' as a symbolic expression of what he explains in another way with the metaphor of a vacuum. He affirms that finitude means that people and the world stand in a complete vacuum, which is to say, that there is 'nothing that can be introduced between the world and God to interpret their relationship'.[17]

The notion of a boundary between God and the world requires explanation. Schillebeeckx unmistakably speaks of a clear distinction or boundary between God and the world of human beings, but the boundary is envisaged from the side of human beings, so to speak, and not from God's. Explained somewhat differently, it is human beings who recognize a frontier between themselves and God. To seek to obliterate such a boundary or distance is the fundamental human sin of idolatry. From God's point of view, as it were, we may imagine that no boundary exists at all since 'God is concerned to be our God in our humanity and for our humanity, in and with our finitude' (IR, p. 115).

THE CREATURE AS GODSELF

The second aspect of creation-faith to be stressed, over and against pantheism, is the conception that although the world and people are entirely other than God, they remain nonetheless within the presence of the divine Creator (GAU, p. 93). When lecturing on creation in Louvain Schillebeeckx made quite a remarkable observation: 'the creature is, in its breadth and depth, *Godself, in a participatory way*.[18] More than three decades later he voiced his conviction that 'in the I–thou relationship between God and humankind God himself includes the human I' (III, p. 100).[19]

Formulations such as these are remarkable in the sense that, although a good deal of late mediaeval Scholastic theology posited a radical bifurcation between infinite and finite beings, Schillebeeckx assumes that being is irreducibly unitary. In other words, he proffers the view that there is only one reality and never two, falsely imagined as separate divine and finite realms: contingent creatures exist *in relation* to divine being. Schillebeeckx's theology of creation, therefore, presupposes an *ontology of relation*: in counterpoise to dualistic ontologies which separate finitude and divinity, Schillebeeckx maintains that reality involves an indivisible relation between God and everything that is finite:

If God, as the belief in God implies, is the absolute meaning of history, there is nothing that can not and must not be related to God. So, everything in reality can become [the] material object of theology, or one can theologize about everything. It is the task of theology to search for that relation between everything and God. In order to do that, the theologian has to accept beforehand that, that relation is present in the objective consistency of every event, independent of whatever awareness that would project that relation into that event.[20]

THE CRITICAL, PRODUCTIVE FORCE OF BELIEF IN CREATION

To move on, Schillebeeckx speaks of creation-faith as having a critical and productive force when he insists that contingent reality can never be absolutized or idolized, or, put differently, that the boundary between God and the non-godly can at no time be surmounted by creatures. The language of a critical and productive force comes from Critical Theory (see pp. 48–51), which hoped to provide an effective conceptual instrument for socio-political change. For Schillebeeckx, the critical force of faith in creation lies in its criticism of overly pessimistic and optimistic conceptions of human history and society. An example of a pessimistic stance would be one that equates any kind of social change with evil. The basic shortcoming of such a perspective is that its negative judgement on change relies on a mistaken view of creation that postulates a good time in the past as a norm for all subsequent history. An example of a faulty optimistic view would be the belief that life and history intrinsically mean progress in themselves. For Schillebeeckx, both views are challenged by creation-faith because, in effect, they are both unhistorical. That is, they ultimately amount to a rejection of the mortality and contingency of social, political and economic forms of history (GAU, p. 97).

Creation-faith is productive in that, by allowing people fully to accept the worth of finitude, it frees them for their own tasks in the world. At this juncture Schillebeeckx's reliance on Irenaeus becomes particularly evident:

> Enjoying and delighting in the secular things of this world, the humanity of man, is enjoying and delighting in what is divine in God. God's honour lies in the happiness and the prosperity of man in the world, who seeks his honour in God: this seems to me to be the best definition of what creation means. In that case this creation is not a single event somewhere in the beginning, but an ongoing dynamic event. God wills to be the origin, here and now, of the worldliness of the world and the humanity of man. He wills to be with us in and with our finite task in the world.[21]

Schillebeeckx's insistence that creation is neither an explanation of the universe's physical composition, nor a source of information about the internal structure of human nature, leads to the possibility of confusion in the way he persists in talking about creation as an *act* of God. The chance of confusion arises here when the action of God is taken to mean that God's activity is to be invoked to explain how matter and biological organisms develop in every detail. However, when Schillebeeckx refers to creation as an action, he refers to *a divine act of trust* in human beings: in creation God establishes secular reality and people in their independence and does not deprive human beings of their responsibility to determine the direction of their contingent lives. Creation, therefore, is God's loving perseverance with that which is finite.

CREATION AND HUMAN FREEDOM

Within Schillebeeckx's understanding of creation, the notion of divine trust ties in with the theme of human freedom, and in so doing rejects a specific conception of predestination. Whereas Hegel once described human history as a slaughter-bench, for Schillebeeckx, it is an adventure: God takes a risk, so to speak, by creating the world, and does not predetermine (as in the theory of predestination) the future of the world. For God, the historical future is unknown. Through creation, God establishes human beings with a contingent free will and thereby allows them to develop their own future. The creation of human beings is thus, as far as God is concerned, a historical risk, adventure, or blank cheque.[22]

The notion of God's trust in secularity has as its corollary the rather extraordinary idea of the vulnerability or powerlessness of God: God does not interfere with the direction of a world whose governance has been given over to human creatures. The concept of God's powerlessness will be central to the immediately forthcoming consideration of creation and the problem of evil.

GOD, CREATION AND THE PROBLEM OF EVIL

At the very least it is arguable that one of the singular causes of atheism in the twentieth century has been the inability of many people to reconcile belief in a creative God and the purported goodness of creation on the one hand, with the demonstrable wretchedness of pervasive human suffering on the other hand. Surely suffering and evil, so the argument unfolds, utterly annul any idea of the goodness of creation. Furthermore, in classical Christian liturgical professions of faith, the idea of creation is linked to God's omnipotence, or unlimited power: 'I believe in God, the Father Almighty, Maker of heaven and earth'. But if God is the all-powerful creator of heaven and earth, whence evil? From God? And why does God abstain from obliterating evil and suffering from the face of the earth?

In explaining to atheistic and religiously sceptical moderns that suffering and evil do not have their source in God as Creator, Schillebeeckx once again betrays the extent to which he stands in a time-honoured theological tradition issuing from Thomas Aquinas. Following Thomas he denies that evil and suffering find a cause or motive in God. The association of suffering and evil with God is, so Schillebeeckx would have it, to a large extent the result of the pervasive and false view that creation is an explanation of how and why the world happens to be as it is. He gives two examples of this view. First, at the beginning of the nineteenth century the practice of inoculation against smallpox was condemned by a Pope on the grounds that the illness was a divine punishment. Second, even today, while the birth of a deformed baby is not necessarily regarded as a divine punishment, it can nevertheless occasionally be interpreted just as misleadingly as a lesson from God.[23]

To counter assumptions like this Schillebeeckx has developed the paradoxical notion of the defencelessness, or the 'defenceless superior power' of God, an idea that has come to the fore only in his more recent works. When he initially mooted the idea he even spoke of the impotence (*onmacht*) of God, but eventually shied away from that term in favour of defencelessness on the grounds that whereas the concepts of power and powerlessness contradict one another, the notion of defencelessness does not necessarily gainsay God's power (see FSG, p. 93). At any rate, the notion of God's defencelessness is an adjunct to the view that God wills to be our God in our finitude. It should be noted in passing that Schillebeeckx's explanation of the notion is indebted to the Dutch theologian Hendrikus Berkhof.

The main reason why Schillebeeckx pursued the notion was to counterbalance the more familiar idea of God's omnipotence and to argue that God does not send suffering upon humans, but works in human history against evil and suffering. Thus, while rejecting the thought that evil finds its cause in God, Schillebeeckx also brushes aside the assumption that God has nothing to do with suffering. On the contrary, he commends the conclusion that

God is actively opposed to suffering: active, that is, through human agents who oppose, where possible, the various causes of suffering. To maintain that God has absolutely nothing to do with suffering, in the sense that God is untouched by human evil, fails to explain adequately how God can be said to be a liberator or saviour. God, therefore, is neither indifferent to, nor the originator of, imperfection and evil (see III, pp. 83–91).

But what, more precisely, does Schillebeeckx mean by the expression of the 'defenceless creator of heaven and earth'? In brief, he means that by giving space, as it were, to human beings, God becomes vulnerable. In his own words:

> To be created is, on the one hand, to be taken up as a creature into God's absolute free and saving nearness, but on the other hand, seen from God's side, it is a sort of 'divine yielding', giving room to the other.[24]

By speaking of God's defencelessness Schillebeeckx does not intend to deny God's immanence in creation. His motive is to assert that God is inwardly present in creation and does not intrude from outside.

Returning to the problem of suffering, it can now be stressed that Schillebeeckx's theology does not attempt to provide an explanation of evil in human history. He does insist, however, that while accounting for an element of chance, our own contingent will can explain why the world looks as it does. Importantly, he asserts that the overcoming of evil in the world is the task of human beings. Yet the surmounting of evil can still be said to involve God to the extent that evil is a human concern and God, as experienced in the Christian tradition, is by nature mindful of humanity (see 1 Timothy 2:1–6; 6:13, 17).

CONCLUSION

To conclude this chapter I reiterate that the most significant aspect of Schillebeeckx's theology of creation is that it is a doctrine *about God*: 'In the depth of everything that is, the mystery of creation and the mystery of God come together in an undivided way'; 'Creation is ultimately the meaning that God has wanted to give to his divine life' (III, pp. 76 and 232). While Christian faith in creation certainly says something about human beings and their world, it is primarily a doctrine which emphasizes that God is involved with humanity and that God does not in any way stand aloof from human contingencies and vagaries. For Schillebeeckx, God is not the 'Wholly Other' of Karl Barth.

In short, Schillebeeckx looks at creation from two different vantage points. From the side of human beings creation means that they are constituted by God in their finitude. But from God's point of view creation is a 'divine yielding', a making room for the non-divine. And it is precisely in this divine yielding that human beings might catch a glimpse, so to say, of God's nature as a love for humankind (*Deus Humanissimus*). God, therefore, is experienceable as transcendent precisely *in* the determinisms of this world.

The manner in which Schillebeeckx speaks about creation reveals him as a markedly anti-dualist and anti-supernaturalist thinker. In this, he is an outstanding Christian intellectual. He is anti-dualist in his refusal to regard reality as a binary thing. With Sartre he can confirm that human existence is irremediably finite. But whereas Sartre describes existence philosophically and exclusively in terms of finitude, Schillebeeckx interprets exactly the same existence theologically in categories of creation. Hence, the selfsame reality is described from two different formal points of view: one is philosophical, the other theological. Schillebeeckx is an anti-supernaturalist theorist in his repudiation of the idea that God could be known in abstraction from, and without association with, human contingency, as if God were remotely contained in some kind of detached supernatural realm. Once again, for Schillebeeckx, God is transcendent in immanence.

That said, it remains to be underscored once more that, as improbable as it may seem, all of Schillebeeckx's explanations of God as creator are collectively and effectively an extended extemporization on a single maxim of Thomas Aquinas, to wit, each and every created thing stands as a constitutive reference to God (*Summa Theologiae*, I, q. 1, a. 7, ad 1). More than that, we may trace Schillebeeckx's fundamental theological lineage much further back in history. His manner of describing creation as a twofold divine action that concurrently establishes creatures in their finitude by inaugurating a history of salvation, and that allows God to be the content of salvation, is nothing if not a recapitulation of St Irenaeus's axiom: *Gloria Dei, vivens homo: vita autem hominis, visio Dei*, which is loosely translatable as 'God's glory or honour lies in the happiness and prosperity of humankind, which in turn, seeks its happiness and honour in God'.

Even while allowing that Schillebeeckx's theology of creation echoes themes of Aquinas and Irenaeus, I would be mischaracterizing it were I to give the impression that it is a simple repetition of their views. Quite the contrary. In saying that his explanations of God as a creator collectively constitute a vast extemporization on one of Aquinas's maxims, I mean just that: they freely and creatively depart from Aquinas even while retaining features of his theology. Even though Schillebeeckx appropriated and developed Aquinas's idea that creatures manifest something of their Creator, and that the world of creation is the only avenue for creaturely knowledge of God, his understanding of creation is also at odds with Aquinas's general view. One would scan Aquinas's works in vain, for example, to discover a notion which is pivotal for Schillebeeckx, namely, the idea that the creation of human beings is, as far as God is concerned, a historical risk, adventure, or blank cheque. Schillebeeckx's notion of God trusting humanity also distances his work from Aquinas. A distinctive aspect of Schillebeeckx's understanding of creation, as I have tried to show, is the imaginative way in which it responds to the work of Sartre and philosophers like him. Occasionally Schillebeeckx's language about God is actually a play on Sartre's words. For instance, if Sartre could say that God is a useless hypothesis, then Schillebeeckx responds by referring to God as a (useless) luxury: 'for believers God is the luxury of their life — our luxury, not so much our cause or final goal, but sheer, superfluous luxury' (JWC, p. 6).

One final remark concerning Schillebeeckx's creation-based theology: it focuses on what I have called the two pillars of Christian faith: belief in God and belief in God's Christ. It explains both pillars in connection with the notion of creation. While the first article of Christian creeds professes a belief in God, Creator of heaven and earth, the second speaks of Jesus Christ, the Son of the Creator. Hence, whereas Schillebeeckx's doctrine of God espouses a *Deus Creator*, his Christology interprets Jesus as concentrated or condensed creation (*verdichte geconcentreerde schepping*): everything that is good in creation is seen most clearly in the figure of Jesus. The meaning of creation as the manifestation of God's nature, as the beginning of salvation, and, in biblical categories, as the inauguration of God's kingdom, receives its amplest clarification in Jesus. And so, it is to Schillebeeckx's Christology that we turn in the next chapter.

Notes

1 The significance of the concept of creation in Schillebeeckx's theology was brought to light in a significant way by the Flemish theologian A. Van de Walle in his article 'Theologie over de Werkelijkheid', *Tijdschrift voor Theologie* 14 (1974), pp. 463–90.

2 For the first seven of these expressions consult III, pp. xviii, 4, 101, 122, and 129. For the penultimate, see GAU, p. 61. The last one appears in JWC, p. 62.

3 Schillebeeckx, *The Eucharist* (London: Sheed & Ward, 1968), p. 147.

4 For example, see I, p. 633; II, pp. 810–11; III, pp. 122, 229–46; FSG, p. 93; JWC, p. 4; and GAU, ch. 16, from where the current chapter takes its title: 'I believe in God, Creator of heaven and earth'.

5 Don Cupitt, 'After liberalism' in D. W. Hardy and P. H. Sedgwick (eds), *The Weight of Glory: A Vision and Practice for Christian Faith: The Future of Liberal Theology: Essays for Peter Baelz* (Edinburgh: T. & T. Clark, 1991), pp. 251–6 (pp. 255–6). The comments made in the above paragraph concerning the philosophy of immanence are based on Yirmiyahu Yovel, *Spinoza and Other Heretics: The Adventures of Immanence* (Princeton, NJ: Princeton University Press, 1989), pp. ix and 167–86.

6 III, p. 234. See p. 77 as well for Schillebeeckx's examples of experiences of radical finitude.

7 A copy of this material is held at the Schillebeeckx Foundation in Nijmegen. Consult, therefore, Edward Schillebeeckx, *Theologische Bezinning op het Scheppingsgeloof*, 2 vols (mimeographed notes; Stichting Edward Schillebeeckx: Katholieke Universiteit Nijmegen, 1956–7), I: 366pp.; II: 330pp.

8   In the first book mentioned, see pp. 91–102. In the second, IR, consult pp. 105–28. And in the third, consider pp. 90–1, and 229–46.

9   For the points made in this and the next two subsections, on emanationism and pantheism, see Schillebeeckx, *Creation*, vol. I, 'Sectio Prima', pp. 2–9; GAU, pp. 91–3, esp. p. 92; and IR, pp. 112–13.

10 See Schillebeeckx, 'God, the Living One', *New Blackfriars* 62:735 (1981), pp. 357–70 (p. 363).

11 For confirmation of these and other points that follow, consult IR, pp. 114–16; and GAU, pp. 94–6.

12 See Schillebeeckx, *Creation*, vol. I, pp. 79A–79B.

13 See MC, p. 139; FSG, p. 93; JWC, pp. 17–18; and III, p. 122.

14 See JWC, pp. 4, 7 and 18; and *Creation*, vol. I, pp. 2 and 84; and vol. II, p. 257.

15 See Edward Schillebeeckx, 'Questions on Christian salvation of and for man' in David Tracy with Hans Küng and Johann B. Metz, *Toward Vatican III: The Work That Needs to Be Done* (New York: Seabury/Concilium, 1978), pp. 27–44, esp. pp. 27–28.

16 See the article which Schillebeeckx wrote to commemorate Metz's sixtieth birthday, 'Befreiende Theologie' in (ed.), *Mystik und Politik: Theologie im Ringen um Geschichte und Gesellschaft* (Mainz: Grünewald, 1988), pp. 56–71 (esp. p. 56).

17 GAU, p. 93. See, in addition, IR, p. 114.

18 Schillebeeckx, *Creation*, vol. I, p. 79B.

19 Schillebeeckx, III, p. 100.

20 Schillebeeckx, 'God, the Living One', pp. 365, and 370, n. 1; parentheses added.

21 IR, pp. 115–16. Schillebeeckx explains his understanding of Irenaeus's expression *Gloria Dei, vivens homo* in *Creation*, vol. II, p. II–407. The expression recurs throughout Schillebeeckx's later publications.

22 The metaphor of a blank cheque is one of Schillebeeckx's favourite figures of speech for elucidating creation. See III, pp. 90–1 and 230–1.

23 See II, p. 729; and GAU, p. 96.

24 FSG, p. 93. For points made immediately above and below, consult as well III, pp. 87 and 231.

6

'I believe in Jesus of Nazareth'

CAN A BABY BE GOD?

In the course of his writings, Edward Schillebeeckx alludes to his infancy and family life with exceptional rarity. When he does, however, his allusions are especially telling, as in the case when he describes children gathered around a Christmas crib:

> When the children cluster round the Crib at Christmas and exclaim in delighted amazement: 'Look, there's the donkey!' 'And there's the star!' 'And that's one of the Three Kings with a present!' 'See the camel?' 'And look, there's Jesus!'—then the believer bows his head . . . 'And there is God'. He, the living God, knows that his immeasurable, all-embracing, matter-of-course presence is impenetrable obscurity for his creatures, and that man therefore longs to meet him somewhere along the way, so that he can point his finger and hear a whisper 'cold' or 'warm' like children at their games when the seeker gets nearer or goes farther away from the place where the thing he is seeking is to be found.[1]

There are no tell-tale indications in this quotation that the reference to children around the crib derives from an incident in Schillebeeckx's own home in Belgium. He explained the incident's significance much later in his life, during an interview he gave to mark his reception of the Erasmus Prize. At the outset of the interview he was asked when he had first heard about Jesus. He replied by telling the story of a Christmas gathering at his home in Kortenberg at the end of World War I. He was about five at the time and remembers his father pointing to the baby in the crib and declaring 'That baby is God!' (see GNM, pp. 1–2).

IS JESUS STILL GOD? YES OR NO?

For the infant Edward, the equation of a baby with God could only appear as indisputable, since it was drawn for him by the authoritative presence of his father. Sixty or so years later, however, he began the epilogue to his book *Interim Report* by recording the question: 'In your view, is Jesus still God? Yes or No?' (p. 140). One reads the epilogue, but a yes-or-no answer is nowhere to be found. As we shall see, Schillebeeckx's accommodation of hermeneutics altered demonstratively his manner of speaking about Jesus and God.

The ensuing chapter provides an interpretation of the essential features of Schillebeeckx's Christology. No attempt is made here to lay bare the length and breadth of his Christology, which runs into thousands of pages. Once again, though, my aim is go to the heart of what he is attempting to achieve with his work, in this instance, by attending to his Christological project.

To that end, I mention the vignette of the crib for two reasons. To begin with, it testifies to what has been a life-long quest for Schillebeeckx: to interpret the sense in which universality can be known in particularity. Expressed theologically, his quest has been to explain how Christian faith enables a believer to contact the reality of God. The image of his father's pointing at the baby as a pointer to God is an image of his entire theological project. As a theologian, in other words, he has attempted to point in God's direction, or to specify the area, terrain, or experience in which God might be met:

> Theology, which claims God himself as its subject, has every reason to be modest nowadays, since everywhere his non-existence is proclaimed as an almost existential experience. As a result we are compelled to circumscribe more exactly the area in which theology, as faith which has become science, establishes contact with the reality of God.[2]

To this day, Schillebeeckx is still to be found talking about aiming or pointing in God's direction: 'God is the reality to which at all events believers point by means of the images of God which are put at their disposal by the history of human religious experience' (III, p. 73). By talking of images aiming at God, Schillebeeckx stands in a long theological tradition. St Gregory of Nyssa (*c.* 330–395), for example, taught that words do not grasp God's reality, but merely aim at the unknown.[3]

My second incentive for mentioning the crib is to draw attention to quite an extraordinary feature of Schillebeeckx's discussions of God, which is, that they are intently focused on the figure of Jesus. His attention to the universality/particularity interchange is grounded most emphatically in the person of Jesus of Nazareth: 'The infinite and the immeasurable have become finite in Christ Jesus. God now stands in our midst in a tangible manifestation, in a form in which we can truly bump into him' (GM, pp. 11–12).

Writing in 1979, Schillebeeckx observed that Jesus raises the issue of God in a period in which many sectors of life appear to do quite well without God. In 1989, he observed that for Christians, Jesus actually defines God: 'God has shown his face in the man Jesus'.[4]

JESUS THE ETHICAL TEACHER

I ought to explain why I call Schillebeeckx's linkage of the question of God with the identity of Jesus quite extraordinary. After all, is it not plainly platitudinous to observe that a Christian theologian concentrates a great deal on Jesus to expound the reality of God? As always, to appreciate why Schillebeeckx theologizes the way he does, it is advisable to attend to philosophical assumptions and intellectual pre-histories that suffuse his theological arguments. His Christology is a clear case in point. I regard the extent to which he broaches the universality/particularity dialectic with attention to Jesus as exceptional in the light of his own attestation that, intellectually, he situates himself in the tradition of the European Enlightenment. While there were certainly several eminent Enlightenment thinkers who sought to rehabilitate Christianity and its faith in Christ philosophically in response to atheistic disavowals of belief in God, there were others bent on unmasking belief in God as an intellectual and human perversion. The point to be borne in mind is that in discussions of God among atheistic thinkers during the heyday of the Enlightenment, Jesus was of no central importance at all. Believers and non-believers alike tended to extol him as an outstanding teacher of ethics. But his own human history was supposed to be of little importance for shedding light on knowledge of God. Never to be underestimated is the extent to which Enlightenment unbelievers or atheists were disgusted and deeply scandalized by the behaviour of Christian churches after the Reformation. Since the sixteenth century, Europe had been ravaged by religious wars. It had witnessed churches organize massacres, excommunicate and burn poor unfortunates in company with ill-starred heretics, and attempt to bring down certain monarchies and post-revolutionary democracies. Christian history, in other words, was blatantly a history of bloodshed, and certainly of no consequence for arriving at indubitable universal knowledge of God. Or so it was thought. Knowledge of God, or of anything else for that matter, could only be affirmed or gainsaid with an appeal to human reason.[5]

Over and against a cluster of post-Enlightenment unbelieving philosophers, therefore, Schillebeeckx persists in talking about God precisely by concentrating on a particular history, namely, the story of Jesus of Nazareth. He insists steadfastly that the only access to knowledge of Jesus, and accordingly of God, is unambiguously through an attention to the tradition and history of Christian churches. In what follows, one of my chief aims is to clarify why Schillebeeckx is unnerved by a specific post-Enlightenment lack of interest in the specific history of Jesus and the historicity of Christianity, and to emphasize that his Christological writings are fired by an overriding problem, which is to explain the ultimate identity of a man, Jesus, as the universal and unique disclosure of divine salvation in human history.

Schillebeeckx's writings on the ultimate import and identity of Jesus are the most gripping—or the most disturbing, depending on one's point of view—in his theological output. In explaining the essential features of his continually evolving Christology, I shall rely mostly on the more important of those writings: *Jesus: An Experiment in Christology* (cited as I); *Christ: The Christian Experience in the Modern World* (II); *Church: The Human Story of God* (III); *Interim Report on the Books 'Jesus' and 'Christ'* (IR); and *Jesus in Our Western Culture* (JWC).

FROM THE GOD-MAN TO THE PROPHET OF GOD

When reading Schillebeeckx's many different books, it soon becomes unmistakably apparent that he speaks of Jesus of Nazareth in starkly different ways. By way of illustration, in his book *Christ the Sacrament*, he describes Jesus as a God-man ('Godmens') (p. 57) and as the central person of the Trinity (pp. 71–2). He concludes that 'Christ is God in a human way, and man in a divine way' (p. 14). And he proposes that the man Jesus is intended by the Father to be the exclusive access to the actuality of redemption (p. 15). In his book on Mary, he maintains that 'Christ is by definition, incarnate God' (p. 81), and that Christ made a painful sacrifice of himself on the cross so as to remove a universal curse hanging over the whole of humankind (p. 51). In short, Schillebeeckx's early writings speak more of Christ than of Jesus; and, incidentally, more of dogma than of history. Importantly, the methodological starting point of his initial Christological inquiries was an acceptance of the dogmatic definition of the Council of Chalcedon (451 CE) according to which, as he points out in *Christ the Sacrament*, 'Christ is "one person in two natures" ' (p. 13). However, Schillebeeckx's later works do not speak of a God-man, but of an eschatological prophet, that is, of a man who preaches an end-time at which God will intervene decisively in human history to humble the exalted and exalt the humbled (see I, pp. 64–74). Quite apart from portraying Jesus as the sole harbinger of, and access to, divine salvation, Schillebeeckx's maturer writings commend the view that 'Jesus not only reveals God but also conceals him' (JWC, p. 2). It follows from this train of thought, then, that other religions apart from Christianity can reveal something of divinely wrought salvation. And again, Schillebeeckx's more recent publications, stopping short of stating plainly that Jesus made a painful sacrifice on the cross to obliterate the deleterious effects of a curse imposed on account of sin, remind their readers that human beings brought Jesus to the cross, not God (JWC, p. 23); that

violence should not be sacralized in God by suggesting that God calls
for a bloody sacrifice on the cross to assuage a divine sense of justice
(see III, p. 125); and that 'we are not redeemed *thanks to* the death
of Jesus but *despite* it' (II, p. 729). When discussing his Christology
in Rome in 1979, Schillebeeckx was asked to clarify what he meant
by the idea that people are saved despite Jesus' death. His reply: 'The
expression "despite his death" means: Despite the execution which
was the doing of men — Jews and Romans — God has not been
checkmated by this occurrence. He took this historical fact into his
plan of salvation' (SC, p. 125).

AFTER CHALCEDON

What explains the varieties of accents and terminology in
Schillebeeckx's early and later accounts of Jesus' identity and uniqueness? In a word, his Christological thinking became markedly
hermeneutical in the latter part of the 1960s, and he became more
aware of the socio-political reaches of Christian faith.

In 1951, Pope Pius XII issued an encyclical entitled *Sempiternus
Rex Christus* ('Everlasting Christ the King'). The encyclical was
published to commemorate the fifteen hundredth anniversary of the
Council of Chalcedon. Revealingly, the Pope reiterated the worth
of Chalcedon's interpretation of Jesus' distinction, and discounted
certain twentieth-century attempts to define Jesus' identity in new
ways. A specific quarry of the Pope was kenotic Christology, that
is, a way of interpreting Jesus' worth according to the category of
his self-giving (kenosis) in life and death.

Within Roman Catholicism, Chalcedon's definition of Jesus'
identity indeed held sway for fifteen centuries. Held sway, that
is, until the Second Vatican Council. In 1943, Pope Pius XII, with
his encyclical *Divino afflante Spiritu* ('On Biblical Inspiration';
literally: 'The Holy Spirit's Breathing'), gave Roman Catholic Scripture scholars permission to use historical methods for biblical
exegesis. The methods had been used to great effect within Protestant biblical scholarship since the nineteenth century. They helped
to obviate fundamentalism in the study of Scripture: fundamentalism here understood as the view according to which a specific
biblical passage is immediately and transparently intelligible
independently of an examination of its specific literary genre or
cultural context. While biblical fundamentalism has long been
recognized as a problem attendant on the interpretation of Scripture, much less adverted to is the pitfall of dogmatic fundamentalism. Before the mid-twentieth century, Catholic dogmatic
theology was hamstrung on two fronts. First, it tended to ignore the
results of exegesis based on historical methods. And second, it was
not sufficiently attentive to the need to interpret dogmas in the light
of their specific historical settings and cultural backcloths.

Of considerable interest in this matter, is that the celebrated
theological schools of Le Saulchoir and Lyon–Fourvière applied

historical methods taken over from biblical studies to shed light on the nature of such topics as the Church and revelation. What they did not do was to apply the methods comprehensively to an interpretation of Jesus Christ. Their shibboleth of 'back to the sources' effectively meant back to the Middle Ages and the late Roman Empire. They did not envisage a return to the times of Jesus and to the most important textual source of all, for Christian theology, namely, the New Testament. As I have suggested before, Schillebeeckx is an outstanding Christian thinker because, in my opinion, he was the first Roman Catholic dogmatician this century to incorporate thoroughly into the mainstream of Catholic dogmatic theology results culled from scientific exegesis. He was certainly not alone in this, but he was arguably pre-eminent.

THE FAITH-CRISIS OF THE 1960s

Part of the crisis of faith that Schillebeeckx diagnosed during his travels in North America involved a Christological component. He records that during his travels he was frequently asked 'Is Christ really God?'[6] Moreover, he recalls that during the 1970s he lectured on Christology in Germany, Belgium, and the Netherlands. Reflecting on his lectures he remembers that whenever he attempted to explain Chalcedon in terms of a divine person functioning 'as person for a human nature', his audiences did not know what he was talking about. He concluded on the basis of his experiences that classical Christology as typified by Chalcedon was largely unintelligible for modern Christians.[7]

That said, it must be noted immediately that Chalcedon is not problematical as far as Schillebeeckx himself is concerned. He once described its view of Jesus Christ as 'pure gospel' (I, p. 35). Just as his theology in general has the pastoral aim of elucidating the meaning of faith in God for those uncertain about God, so too his more recent Christology strives to clarify the meaning of belief in Jesus Christ for those needled by uncertainties in the midst of secularization and conceptual pluralism.

'SWALLOW IT OR CHOKE'

Schillebeeckx changed the method he used in Christology once he perceived that many moderns could not understand a particular dogmatic definition of Jesus Christ. Rather than basing his Christological researches primarily on Chalcedon's definition, he began instead with an examination of Christian origins. Despite its esteemed history in theology, Chalcedon is not the primary source for Christology. It relied, understandably enough for its time, on Graeco-Roman philosophical concepts in order to express its faith. However, the ultimate criterion for reinterpretations of faith is not Greek philosophy, or any other philosophy for that matter. It will be recalled that in the midst of faith-crises in the 1960s, Schillebeeckx pointed out that the measuring-rod for calibrating the authenticity of a reinterpretation of faith is not a particular doctrine but the reality referred to by doctrines. In the context of a Christological crisis of faith he engaged exactly the same axiom he had taken over from Aquinas: The act of the believer terminates at the reality of God and not at statements about God. Thus, the focus of Schillebeeckx's later works on Jesus was not on dogma, but on the figure of Jesus himself as he is spoken of and remembered in the New Testament and early Christian tradition. When Schillebeeckx embarked on a study of hermeneutics in 1966, his first significant application of hermeneutical theory and biblical exegesis was in his book *Jesus* (1974). With the publication of that book he effectively announced a new understanding of the conditions for confessing faith in the modern world. He explains, in a book commenting on the first two parts of his Christological trilogy, that in present-day circumstances people will no longer accept Christian faith purely on the authority of others. In other words, handing on faith is no longer a matter, as he says, of 'Swallow it or choke' (IR, pp. 4 and 6). Faith will only be professed if it becomes intelligible in the light of current experiences and patterns of thought. Simple repetition of past dogmas is not coextensive with efficacious transmission of faith. Dogmas, like any texts from the past, need to be interpreted hermeneutically. That is to say, they are rendered more intelligible if they are examined in the dual lights of their historical contexts and of contemporary patterns of comprehension. Theology, then, has two cardinal sources, not one. Thus has it always been. Along with the entire Christian tradition stands a second source, contemporary experiences: 'no one is in a position to rediscover precisely what the message of the gospel now means to us, except in relation to our present situation' (IR, p. 3). Unmistakably, Schillebeeckx's later Christology regards present-day experiences as 'an intrinsic and determinative element for understanding God's revelation in the history of Israel and of Jesus . . .' (ibid.).

Hitherto, I have been commenting in broad terms on Schillebeeckx's Christological turnabout, as it were, and on twentieth-century Roman Catholic developments in Christology. Before moving on to consider the characteristics of Schillebeeckx's Christological project, two matters remain to be touched upon. The first concerns the principal intellectual dilemmas with which his large books on Jesus grapple. The second concentrates on the early phases of his Jesus-quest.

THE CHALLENGE OF LESSING

At this stage I rely once again on my suggestion that a useful way of pinpointing the central preoccupation of an outstanding thinker is to pose the question: Who or what is this thinker arguing against, and what is this thinker arguing for?

As a university discipline, theology has an eight-hundred-year-old history. However, that history can be divided into two major periods: the past two hundred years, and the six hundred antedating them. The watershed dividing the two was the intellectual upheaval brought about by the Enlightenment, and the separation between the two has been most evident in Protestant circles. It was only after the waning of Neo-Scholasticism in the wake of Vatican II that Catholic scholars in large numbers reflected post-Enlightenment theological concerns in their deliberations. In bare summary, modern theologies are distinguishable from pre-Enlightenment ones by a resolute acknowledgement of the historical variability and limitation of all human knowledge.[8]

In the eighteenth century, a German writer, Gotthold Ephraim Lessing (1729–81), repudiated past history as a source for reliable knowledge. For Lessing, a particular historical experience cannot furnish knowledge of that which is universal. We notice at once that Lessing announces a pressing challenge for Schillebeeckx, who hopes to demonstrate that the man Jesus, a contingent figure in history, was and is the revelation of universal knowledge of God.

Lessing introduced one of the most oft-quoted non-biblical metaphors of the past two centuries into Protestant theology. His metaphor was that of an ugly ditch. In a seminal essay 'On the proof of the spirit and of power' (1777) he discoursed on the attempt to prove the truth of Christianity, especially with recourse to historical means. He conceded that were he personally to have seen Jesus perform miracles (the proof of power), or had he been able to see prophecies fulfilled by Jesus (the proof of the spirit), then of course he could accept the truth of Christianity. However, he maintained that miracles no longer happen. Consequently, references to miracles in the first Christian century do nothing to establish the veracity of Christianity for moderns who no longer experience them. Moreover, according to Lessing, nothing can be demonstrated by means of historical truths if no historical truth can be demonstrated: 'That, then, is the ugly, broad ditch which I cannot get across, however often and however earnestly I have tried to make the leap'.[9] Lessing's basic intent in speaking of a broad ugly ditch was to proffer the view that affirmations of faith cannot be drawn from historical events. The language of history and the language of faith are two different planes of discourse. To attempt to move from one to the other is to strive to jump over a ditch. For example, the claim that Jesus is the pre-eminent revelation of God is an attestation of faith, but it cannot be authenticated on the basis of particular historical data.

Now the problem or challenge which Lessing's work posed for Schillebeeckx was the idea that no individual historical particularity can be called absolute (see III, p. 166). And yet, that is precisely what Schillebeeckx's maturer theology seeks to countenance. Or more exactly, it strives to illustrate that something of the absolute can indeed be localized in a historical particularity like Jesus of Nazareth. That is all well and good, yet Schillebeeckx did not respond to Lessing until the 1970s and afterwards. We shall attend to his response in due course and ask if it is adequate. But for the moment, we leave that challenge in abeyance to describe Schillebeeckx's early Christology which is a prelude to and preparation for the later.

A HUMAN PERSON OF DIVINE NATURE

One of the major courses Schillebeeckx conducted in Louvain after his studies in France was in the field of Christology. As with his course on creation, the Christology lecture notes that he distributed among his students are replete with clues for coming to grips with his major intellectual preoccupations. And similarly, while there are elements of change and permanence in his overall theology, so too there are abiding and variable interests and themes in his Christological inquiries.

I have previously ventured the view that Schillebeeckx's theology is a vast excursus on a single text of St Thomas (*Summa Theologiae*, I, q. 1, a. 7, ad 1). In exactly the same vein I would advance the suggestion that from beginning to end, his Christology has been an attempt to expound and explore the implications of another text by Aquinas found in the *Summa Theologiae*: III, q. 2, a. 10. Schillebeeckx addresses the text in his Louvain lectures on Christology. There he explains that the text in question has a disputed history. In a majority of manuscripts, Thomas is represented as elaborating on Christ as someone in whom human nature is assumed in such a way as *to be the person* of the Son of God ('in quo humana natura assumpta est ad hoc quod sit *persona* Filii Dei'). The Leonine edition of Aquinas's works, that is, the edition commissioned by Pope Leo XIII, offers a different rendering by stating that human nature is assumed in Christ so as *to belong to the person* of the Son of God ('in quo humana natura assumpta est ad hoc quod sit *personae* Filii Dei'). The difference is capital, since the first, majority reading suggests that Aquinas held that Jesus' humanity *is itself* the manner of the Son of God's being. Christ, then, is a human person of divine nature. The Leonine version, however, intimates that Christ's humanity belongs to the divine person of the Son.[10]

While teaching in Louvain, Schillebeeckx regarded the notion that Jesus is God as a methodological point of departure. Explicitly approving of Chalcedon, he interpreted Jesus in terms of his divine and human natures. Even so, he made clear that Jesus is not a human person standing next to a divine person. Relying on Aquinas, he tried to take full cognizance of Jesus' humanity by stressing that the humanity is the Son of God's manner of being.

NIJMEGEN'S DEBATE ON JESUS

I noted above that 1966 was a crucial period for Schillebeeckx's intellectual history. Apart from his first trip to the United States of

America, and his initiation into hermeneutics at the Catholic University of Nijmegen, 1966 also signposted another major development in his thought, especially with respect to Christology.

During 1966, the Dutch theological review *Tijdschrift voor Theologie* devoted an entire issue to the significance of Jesus Christ. The issue bore the title *Gods heilspresentie in de mens Jezus* ('God's saving presence in the man Jesus'), and contained articles by three professors: Ansfried Hulsbosch, Edward Schillebeeckx and Piet Schoonenberg (b. 1911). Hulsbosch taught scripture and theology in Nijmegen, while Schoonenberg was the professor of theology for undergraduates. Schillebeeckx held the chair in theology and the history of theology for postgraduate students.

The work of Hulsbosch illustrates amply just how essential it is to attempt to pinpoint the precise intellectual currents that Schillebeeckx met at first hand during his career; currents that helped shape the development of his ideas. Hulsbosch, like De Petter, is not a well-known figure to English-speakers. Schoonenberg, on the other hand, has been widely translated into English. Yet Hulsbosch, a Dutch Augustinian friar, triggered an important change in Schillebeeckx's reflections on the ultimate identity and universal significance of Jesus of Nazareth.

So what is it that Hulsbosch saw that so affected Schillebeeckx? Like Schillebeeckx, Hulsbosch had once accepted that Christian faith in Christ could be adequately expounded in the latter part of the twentieth century with the aid of Chalcedon. With his article of 1966, however, he made the somewhat daring suggestion that classical Catholic Christology was dualistic, that is, it dichotomized Jesus Christ into two components: one divine, the other human; one a transcendent divinity, the other a historical humanity. If dualism is unacceptable in anthropology, then Hulsbosch argued that it is unacceptable in Christology. The significance of his essay, entitled 'Jesus Christ, known as man, professed as Son of God', was its assertion that the humanity of Jesus is the unique mediation of divine revelation and that the entire mystery of the revelation of salvation in Jesus is located in his humanity.[11] Hulsbosch was not at all concerned to discard the age-old quest to locate a nexus between the divine and the human in Jesus. What he would not brook was the idea that the identity of Jesus was binary, with human and divine constituents. In the long run, the real significance of Hulsbosch's work was that he advocated a more hermeneutical approach to Christological discussion. Whereas a non-hermeneutical thinker would suppose that the assertion 'Jesus is truly God and truly human' is immediately intelligible, a more hermeneutically predisposed thinker would immediately seek clarifications: Christian tradition subscribes to the view that God is Trinitarian, yet Jesus is not Trinitarian. So how can Jesus be called 'God'? And again, what is 'God' or 'humanity' in any case? Before enjoining that Jesus is God and human, at the very least the terms 'God' and 'humanity' need to be clarified.

Interestingly, Schoonenberg responded to Hulsbosch by declaring that he was uncertain as to whether the Chalcedonian definition of Christ needed to be retained for the purposes of specifying the authenticity of Christian belief and the uniqueness of Christ. Schillebeeckx's response, in an article called 'Personal revelation-figure of the Father', subscribed to the view that it is necessary to retain the notion of 'hypostasis' in Christology. To explain that term 'hypostasis': Chalcedon's interpretation of Jesus is frequently summarized in association with the theory of 'hypostatic union', the words 'hypostatic' and 'hypostasis' being Hellenized ways of talking about *natures*. A hypostatic union is a fusion of two natures. The theory of hypostatic union surmises that a divine and human nature cohere in the person of Christ. The noteworthy facet of Schillebeeckx's response to Hulsbosch is that he lauded the latter's inclination to supersede a dualistic Christology. And so, Schillebeeckx declared that since 1953, he had always been opposed to the theological formula 'Christ is God and man', and also against the formula that 'the man Jesus is God'. He preferred to speak, so he said, of Jesus the Christ, who is the Son of God *in humanity*. Rather than adopting the ancient formula 'hypostatic *union*', Schillebeeckx propounded a theory of 'hypostatic *unity*': the difference being for him that the word 'unity' does not necessarily suggest that Jesus' identity includes two separate parts.[12]

Lest it be suspected that I am inflating Hulsbosch's influence on Schillebeeckx, I emphasize once again that the former's article was entitled 'Jesus Christ, known as man, professed as Son of God'. Hulsbosch's title expresses full well exactly the same point made by Lessing: historical discourse is not the same as faith-discourse. Hence, something of Jesus might be known through the exigencies of human history; and on another plane, he could be lauded as the beloved of God. Twenty-two years after dissecting Hulsbosch's article, Schillebeeckx is still to be found speaking of Jesus' historical way of living that enables him to be confessed as the Christ.[13]

REVAMPING CHRISTOLOGY: ACCESS TO JESUS OF NAZARETH

We move on now to consider the features of Schillebeeckx's later, post-1950s and 1960s Christology. After his excursions into hermeneutics, his travels in North America, and his discussions with Hulsbosch and Schoonenberg, he set to work to write a new Christology. The first fruits of his labours appeared in 1972 in an article called, in the Dutch, 'Access to Jesus of Nazareth'.[14]

There are a number of important features to note regarding this text. To begin with, it reveals a relatively new conversance on the part of Schillebeeckx with the two-centuries-long history of modern historical research into the identity of Jesus. In the article, Schillebeeckx traces the development of the Old and New Quests of the historical Jesus. Since the 1970s, his own researches have stood in line with the New Quest. To elaborate a little, critical historical research into Jesus is customarily concluded to have begun in 1778, with the posthumous publication of a text by the German professor of Oriental languages at Hamburg, Hermann Samuel Reimarus (1694–1768). The text in question, 'On the intention of Jesus and his disciples', drew a distinction between the Jesus of history and the Christ of faith, which has since become standard in a good deal of Christology. The publication of Reimarus's work launched what has come to be known as the Old Quest of, or for, the historical Jesus. That quest was impelled in a significant way by the publication in 1835–36 of David Friedrich Strauss's (1808–74) book *Leben Jesu* (Eng. trans. *The Life of Jesus Critically Examined*). Both Reimarus and Strauss surmised that the New Testament gospels are untrustworthy documents for providing historical information concerning Jesus. For Reimarus, they were fabrications concocted by Jesus' followers. For Strauss, they were the accretions of poetic mythology.

And so, the Old Quest (*c.* 1778–1906) gave way to a period (1906–53) when there was little sustained attempt in European academic circles to gather historical information concerning Jesus. Rudolf Bultmann (1884–1976) typifies the prevailing view of this period that historical research does not legitimate faith in Christ and that it is methodologically unfeasible to write a life of Jesus based on historical research.

In 1953, however, Ernst Käsemann (b. 1906), a pupil of Bultmann, effectively launched a New Quest of the historical Jesus by qualifying the historical scepticism of the Old Quest. Käsemann was of the opinion that while the gospels are from beginning to end works of theological proclamation and not historical reportage, they nonetheless refer to a person in history.

Another noteworthy feature of Schillebeeckx's article 'Access to Jesus of Nazareth' is that he speaks of the importance of what he calls thinking in models (pp. 30–2). He means by this that theories or models of thought have a certain primacy with respect to particular experiences. Hence, all religious and biblical statements are made not on the basis of raw, uninterpreted experiences, but through the filter of pre-established theoretical models. While this matter may seem slightly abstruse, it is an epistemological stance of considerable consequence for shaping Schillebeeckx's later Christology. Recognizing the primacy of models in thought, Schillebeeckx observes that successive generations of Christians have interpreted Jesus with recourse to dissimilar models or titles, such as 'Christ', 'Son of Man', or 'Lord'. The point to be retained is that for Schillebeeckx, titles are of secondary importance. In attempting to interpret Jesus, Jesus himself is the pre-eminent factor (p. 36).

Lest it be thought, however, that Schillebeeckx founds his revamped Christology on an attempt to gain access to the historical identity of Jesus by way of historical-critical methods, a major feature of the article presently under consideration is its author's conclusion that access to Jesus of Nazareth is by way of the movement or community that gathered in his name after his death. In other words, an approach to Jesus is mediated through the Church (pp. 44–6 and 59).

One final remark: the article also clarifies a distinction between the 'historical Jesus' (*historische Jezus*) and the 'earthly or natural Jesus' (*aardse Jezus*). The former expression designates that image of Jesus that can be reconstructed with historical methods. But it is no more than an image, because the Jesus who lived in Galilee (the natural Jesus) can never be recovered by historical methodology.

JESUS, THE STORY OF THE LIVING ONE

The points sketched above received a far ampler exposition in 1974 with the publication of the first part of Schillebeeckx's trilogy of books on Jesus. The original Dutch title, translatable as *Jesus, the Story of One Alive*, traded on a grammatical ambiguity: Was the story in question told by Jesus himself, or was it another's narration about him? In any event, from beginning to end the treatise is concerned with the actual identity of Jesus, insofar as that might be reconstructed by historical criticism and analysis of the historical genesis of Christian faith (I, p. 34).

The book has a fourfold structure. Its first part discusses matters of method and hermeneutics pertaining to contemporary Christological investigations (pp. 41–104). The second part undertakes a detailed reading of New Testament texts with a view to extruding historical data concerning Jesus (pp. 105–397). The third moves on to an analysis of early Christian interpretations of Jesus (pp. 399–571), while the fourth responds to the question of what Jesus might mean for present-day Christians (pp. 573–674). The third part is motivated by the conviction that in order to ascertain more of the identity of Jesus with the aid of historical-critical methods, it is necessary to attend to the 'horizon of experience', or cultural context, in which the first Jews and Gentiles interpreted Jesus (see p. 102).

The method employed in the first Jesus book is highly original. The book was not designed as a conventional treatise in Christology, but as a prolusion or prolegomenon to a full-grown Christology. Schillebeeckx called his method a *manuductio* (*handleiding*). By attempting to reconstruct Christian origins, and to trace the genesis of faith in Jesus, he wished to take his readers by the hand (*manuductio*), so to speak, on a journey back to Palestine, to see what historical-exegetical studies have to say about Jesus' life there, and then to accompany Jesus' disciples on the way they came to express faith in him after his death.[15]

JUSTICE AND LOVE; GRACE AND LIBERATION

The second part of the trilogy, *Justice and Love; Grace and Liberation* (to translate its more revealing Dutch title), appeared in 1977, and was even longer than the first. Unlike the initial volume in the Jesus-project, the second was not directly concerned with the identity of Jesus as it is reconstructed provisionally and partially by historical methods. Instead, it examined New Testament theologies of grace, that is, theologies concerning the manner in which God's presence is perceived by Christians. While the first volume used historical-critical methods, the second used literary methods to analyse New Testament texts.

Be it noted, however, that both books share a similar structure, since the second also has four major divisions, the largest of which is an examination of New Testament texts. Hence, the first part considers the notion of experience and the interplay between New Testament and contemporary experiences (II, pp. 27–79). The second pores over New Testament theologies of the experience of grace (pp. 81–627). The third, very short, part extracts what Schillebeeckx regards as the structural elements, or absolute basics, of the New Testament theologies of grace (pp. 629–44). The fourth part analyses contemporary human experiences in the light of which Schillebeeckx tries his hand at elaborating a contemporary theology of grace (pp. 645–839). In the fourth division, therefore, Schillebeeckx attempts to achieve theologically what New Testament authors did in their own times. The book ends with an epilogue, some prayers, and a profession of faith (pp. 840–52). At the outset of the epilogue Schillebeeckx explains that he had originally intended to end the volume with discussion on the Holy Spirit and the Church. Because the book had assumed large proportions he was not able to fulfil his original plan. A third volume was already in sight.

For all its size and complication, the second instalment in the trilogy is driven by two major aims. First, to understand the manner in which the earliest New Testament witness to Christian faith explained the way divine salvation is localized in the figure of Jesus. And second, to probe the extent to which the New Testament witnesses provide a normative orientation for contemporary Christians in their own interpretations of Jesus' salvific relevance (see p. 24).

RULERS AND THE RULED

After all the biblical analysis undertaken in the third part of the second volume, Schillebeeckx pauses to make a pregnant remark. He confesses that the words of Luke's Jesus keep ringing in his ears. He then refers to a text in the Gospel according to Luke (22: 25–26a) where Christians are told that they are not to exercise lordship over others. He goes on to remark:

This saying puts everyone to shame, unfortunately including Christianity, which since the fourth century (despite constant marginal protests at every level which have gone unnoticed) has succumbed to the temptation to exercise this worldly power and has done what 'the world' does, despite its sayings directed against the world. (p. 648)

What this text indicates is that Schillebeeckx's Christological trilogy is styled as a theology of liberation for contemporary Westerners. By a theology of liberation, I mean a way of talking about God which underscores an ancient biblical image of God as One who works in human history, through prophets and martyrs, to overturn the subjugation of the weak at the hands of society's powerful. Writing in 1973, Schillebeeckx professed that 'in contemporary society it is impossible to believe in a Christianity that is not one with the movement to emancipate mankind'.[16]

Warming to his theme in *Justice and Love; Grace and Liberation*, Schillebeeckx points out that:

The biblical vision of the coming kingdom of God envisages a humanity in which there are no more exploiters and no more exploited humanity, no more individual or structural servitude and no more slaves. For that reason God's will to salvation is universal. (II, pp. 651–2)

CHRISTIANITY HUMANIZES RELIGION AND THE WORLD

I have quite deliberately retained a close translation of the Dutch title of the second part of Schillebeeckx's trilogy to highlight its cardinal underlying theme. As I have said, the book is a tract on grace. Technically, the reality of God is not the same thing as a human experience of God's grace. The latter involves an experience of God's presence among human beings, whereas the former is not limited by human perceptions of God. For all we know, God could well be present to others elsewhere, outside, as it were, the orbit of human history. The title of the second volume is revealing in that it obviates a dualism of grace. I have stressed before that Schillebeeckx is a profoundly anti-dualistic thinker. In Christology, he refuses to speak of Jesus in terms of two component parts. The reality of Jesus is hereby taken to be unitary: with an anthropological language he is spoken of as a man; yet with religious language one can speak of his divinity. So too, with regard to grace, Schillebeeckx is decidedly anti-dualistic. Note, therefore, that the words 'grace' and 'liberation' have different provenances. Grace is used primarily in religious and theological contexts, whereas liberation is not such a specifically religious term and has socio-political resonances as well. Now the point is this:

If anywhere in theology there is any question of pseudo-problems piling up, then it is precisely in the field of the relationship to all these cases in which human reality and the reality of grace — like, for example, freedom and grace; emancipatory self-liberation and Christian redemption; the humanity and divinity of Jesus — are set side by side and alongside each other as two different realities which on this presupposition must subsequently be reconciled dialectically by all kinds of theological devices. (III, p. 211)

In short, for Schillebeeckx, a social-political movement attempting to humanize subhuman situations is itself a form of grace (see GNM, p. 100).

JESUS IN OUR WESTERN CULTURE

Three years before the publication of the third part of the trilogy, Schillebeeckx released a short work in which he prefigured many of the major preoccupations of the third part. Suffice it to record at this stage that the small book, translated in English as *Jesus in Our Western Culture*, perpetuates a reigning preoccupation of the first two volumes, that is, to sketch a Western theology of liberation by illustrating that to humanize society is to experience God's grace. *Jesus in Our Western Culture* shows that faith, as far as Schillebeeckx is concerned, is a multiplex reality: it has mystical, socio-political, ethical, ecological, and inter-personal dimensions (JWC, p. 65). The political dimension of faith is misrepresented if understood as political party partisanship, or full-time direction of state government. In Schillebeeckx's eyes, politics means 'an intensive form of social commitment' (ibid., p. 72). To be political is to seek to humanize society. In addition to elucidating the political aspect of Christian faith, the book attests that, as far as its author is concerned:

The most obvious, modern way to God is that of welcoming fellow human beings, both interpersonally and by changing structures which enslave them. . . . God is accessible above all in the praxis of justice: 'No one has ever seen God; if we love one another, God abides in us and his love is perfected in us' (I John 4. 12). (Ibid., pp. 63–4)

HUMAN BEINGS AS GOD'S STORY

The final offering in the trilogy is much shorter than the first two. It does not add significantly to the exegetical material deployed in the first part, penned some fifteen years earlier. In this, the book is something of a disappointment. To provide just one justification for the comment made in the last sentence, Schillebeeckx's trilogy, including its last part, fully recognizes that Jesus was a Jew, and that the first Christians were Jews (III, pp. 147–54). The third part of the trilogy, however, could have availed itself of recent studies that clarify more precisely the nature of the Jewish circles in which Jesus lived, that is, the Judaism of Galilee.[17]

Be that as it may, one of the strengths of the third volume is that it presents Schillebeeckx's Christological thought in summary and orderly fashion. The book has five chapters. The first sketches a theology of revelation (pp. 1–45). The second broaches the topic of the conditions for believing in, and talking about, God in the late twentieth century (pp. 46–101). The third concerns Christology (pp. 102–86), and is really the central division of the work. The fourth discusses the Church (pp. 187–228), and the fifth asks whether the Church has a future in an ecologically preoccupied age, and re-articulates its author's theology of creation (pp. 229–46).

A word of warning: This book is expressed in a simpler language than the first two parts of the trilogy, but its content is nevertheless tightly compact. Many of its pages require several readings to arrive at an appreciation of what the author is seeking to communicate.

SCHILLEBEECKX'S CHRISTOLOGY IN A NUTSHELL

Having surveyed Schillebeeckx's major studies of Jesus' ultimate significance, I should now like to draw together the threads of his studies to accentuate the major characteristics of his mature Christology and to illustrate the way he responds to the challenge typified by Lessing.

(a) The eschatological prophet

The first point I would make in this context is that Schillebeeckx's own preferred image or model for interpreting Jesus is that of a prophet. A prophet is not here understood as a foreteller of the future, but as one who is acutely alive to current realities of suffering. Moreover, for Schillebeeckx, Jesus is an eschatological prophet, a prophet of the end-time, and:

> The man who so intensely recalls the history of human suffering and sees it in such concentrated form as an excessive accumulation of hurt and unrelieved suffering that he is convinced that the measure is so full that something definitively new just has to happen. (GAU, p. 34)

Right at the end of the first Jesus book Schillebeeckx has this to say:

> Whereas God is bent on showing himself in human form, we on our side slip past this human aspect as quickly as we can in order to admire a 'divine Ikon' from which every trait of the critical prophet has been smoothed away. (I, p. 671)

Despite variations and qualifications, all three parts of the trilogy interpret the life, career, message, death, and professed resurrection, along similar lines. It is important to observe that Schillebeeckx insists that neither the life, death, nor resurrection of Jesus can be understood in isolation. That is, his life sheds light on the meaning of his death and resurrection, as these last two reflect on his life. It should be noted immediately, too, that talk of Jesus' resurrection is not of the same order as speech concerning his life and death, for the resurrection is a theological concept referring to an event, although not to a normally and historically observable event.

(b) Proclamation and conduct

As for the career, conduct and message of Jesus, Schillebeeckx accepts the findings of recent biblical scholarship that the centre of Jesus' life and preaching was a message concerning the kingdom of God. For Schillebeeckx, the phrase 'kingdom of God' refers to God's actual nature. Jesus' stories or parables about the kingdom, therefore, explicate God's nature. Moreover, a striking feature of Jesus' conduct, for Schillebeeckx, is that it cohered with his message about the kingdom. In other words, Jesus' actions directly rendered intelligible what he was preaching about. More than that, the nature of the kingdom is tied up with the figure of Jesus: 'Jesus acts as God acts' (JWC, p. 20).

I said above that Schillebeeckx's Christological writings contain some of his most gripping—or unsettling—prose. This is especially the case when he speaks of God's kingdom. He regards Jesus' message of the kingdom as a proclamation of the humanity of God (see FSG, p. 48). The kingdom of God, never completely definable, is the saving presence of God made manifest in human beings' abolition of blatant contrasts between rulers and the ruled (see III, pp. 111–12). Jesus' parables:

> teach us that God does not mean to be a guarantor of privileged positions in bourgeois or religious society. . . . In the parables Jesus shows 'the other face of religion (or the church)': his [God's] way of being the 'God of men and women', of all men and women, makes him primarily the God of the outcast and the excluded. Anyone who cannot hear that from the New Testament, above all in the parables, has understood nothing of Jesus's message of the kingdom of God. (Ibid., p. 115)

So much for Jesus' proclamation of God's reign. Schillebeeckx also speaks of Jesus' actions in accord with his kingdom-preaching. When he does so, Schillebeeckx gives a clearer indication of what he means by the ever-present word 'praxis' in his theology. Thus, Jesus' praxis of the kingdom of God, and any Christian's emulative praxis, is an alternative mode of action. Alternative, that is, in comparison to the behaviour of those who enslave society's cast-offs and pariahs:

> For Jesus, the praxis of the kingdom of God seems to be alternative action, in contrast to what people are usually inclined to do in our society. Jesus does not defend people who do evil, but he does go and stand beside them. He unmasks the intentions of those who are zealous for God and justice when they do not act for the salvation and well-being of others, but to the detriment of human beings, men and women. Insisting on rights can in fact include the excommunication of people who have already been outcast, in whose case there is whispering behind their backs: '. . . divorced, homosexual, heretic, married priest!' (FSG, p.18).

The word 'praxis', a neologism in English, connotes an indivisible interplay between an action and a theory. An action in itself is not auto-justificatory. Nazism, for example, is a political mode of action, but it is not immediately recognizable, to say the least, as a just and worthwhile form of action. Hence, social, political, and religious actions need some kind of guiding theory, or Archimedean measuring-rod, against which the legitimacy and worth of an action can be calculated. For Schillebeeckx, that measuring-rod is Jesus' proclamation of God's kingdom. Christian praxis, therefore, is a praxis of the kingdom. As such, it has two facets. In the first place, it is a refusal, in actions and words, of oppressive power. Secondly, it is an acceptance of the consequences of a life spent in service of the socially cold-shouldered. Praxis, then, is resistance and surrender; following Jesus (*sequela Jesu*); and a way of the cross (*via crucis*). This way of speaking about praxis is, of course, highly reminiscent of Dietrich Bonhoeffer (1906–45).

(c) Jesus' death

The first thing that can be said, therefore, in interpreting Jesus' death, is that it was a consequence of his way of life: a life in unremitting service of justice and love, a consequence of an option for the outcast and destitute, and a choice for people suppurating under exploitation (see III, p. 125). Moreover, it was a premature death, a death by execution. Like God, Jesus identified with society's human refuse, and the unholy (see IR, p. 132). His death was not the folly of a spontaneous lynching party, but the consequence of a decision made by religious and political authorities to get rid of him. For segments of the religious ruling class in Jerusalem at the time of Jesus' death, his preaching was a prophetic accusation. For the Roman prefect in Jerusalem, and for the Roman occupying powers in Palestine, his message of the kingdom, and its accompanying praxis, was a frontal condemnation: 'Jesus said, You know that the kings of the Gentiles exercise lordship over them; and those in authority over them are called benefactors. But not so with you

(Luke 22: 25)' (quoted ibid.). Consequently, it was not God, 'but men and women who put Jesus to death' (III, pp. 126–7).

(d) Jesus' resurrection and appearances

In 1974 Schillebeeckx proposed a novel interpretation of Jesus' resurrection (I, pp. 320–402; 516–44; 644–50). It drew considerable criticism from some quarters. In brief, he hypothesized that some-time after Jesus' death, his erstwhile disciples, who had fled in fear after his death, eventually regrouped and began preaching that Jesus had been raised from death. But what made them regroup? According to Schillebeeckx's theory, they underwent an experience of forgiveness and conversion. The source of their experience of forgiveness was, so the argument goes, the Risen Jesus, since a dead person cannot proffer forgiveness.

Schillebeeckx's hypothesis is simply that: a hypothesis. The more interesting aspect of his analysis of Christian faith in the resurrection of Jesus has to do with the New Testament accounts of the risen Lord's appearances after the resurrection. In discussions of Schillebeeckx's interpretation of the resurrection, insufficient atten-tion has been given to the epistemological theory that undergirds his approach. The New Testament contains a central formula according to which Jesus appeared to his followers after his resurrection: see, for example, 1 Corinthians 15: 3–6a. In what sense, though, is the phrase 'he appeared' to be taken? Does it refer to a visual phenomenon, an ocular perception, or some kind of personal revelation of truth?

Schillebeeckx interprets the appearances in a way quite different from Aquinas. The latter stressed the visibility and palpability of the risen Lord by asserting that Jesus' followers saw with their own eyes the living Christ whom they knew to have died (*Summa Theologiae*, III, q. 55, a. 2), and that flesh, bones, blood and other elements pertain to the nature of Christ's risen body (*Summa Theologiae*, III, q. 54, a. 3). Schillebeeckx, on the other hand, places his emphasis elsewhere. He does not stress that the appear-ances of the risen One *necessarily* involved sense-perception (at least, not in some naïve realistic sense) on the part of those to whom Christ is believed to have appeared. Schillebeeckx rejects the notion, correctly in my judgement, that the empirical establishment of a physically visible Jesus need be the *foundation* of Christian belief (see IR, p. 82). For Schillebeeckx, in a manifestation of the Risen Christ, it would not have been necessary for Jesus to have been seen in a visual sense (I, p. 369). And so, 'seeing' through faith need not necessarily involve seeing!

Furthermore, Thomas argued that Christ appeared to his disciples in order *to engender* faith concerning the resurrection. In other words, he interpreted sensory appearances as motives for faith-credibility (*Summa Theologiae*, III, q. 55, a. 3). Schillebeeckx, on the other hand, maintains that an Easter appearance is not the object of a neutral observation, but a faith-motivated experience *in response* to an eschatological disclosure (I, p. 378). Clearly, for Aquinas, resurrection appearances precede and *cause* faith; for Schillebeeckx, they are consequent upon and *confirm* faith.

The primary mistake made in criticisms of Schillebeeckx's interpretations of the resurrection and the appearances is the claim that he denies Jesus' bodily and personal resurrection. Quite the opposite is the case: he openly confirms a bodily-cum-personal resurrection on the part of Jesus (I, pp. 644–50; and IR, p. 83). He maintains that the resurrection is a real event, accomplished by God in Jesus. Nonetheless, as reality, it is meta-empirical, meta-historical, and eschatological. All of which is to assert, that what the resurrection involved, if it involved God, cannot be adequately imagined within the confines of human language and history. The unacknowledged subtlety in Schillebeeckx's entire discussion of Christian faith in the resurrection is simply this: he applies Edmund Husserl's principle of the intentionality of consciousness to interpret resurrection faith. And so, he distinguishes objective and subjective elements in resurrection faith. The objective pole consists in Jesus' personal and corporeal resurrection and exaltation with God (IR, p. 79: I, pp. 644–5). The subjective element is said to be the experience of faith which is expressed in Scripture in the stories of the appearances (IR, p. 79). Not only does Schillebeeckx distinguish these two elements; he also concludes that they are inseparable:

> Without the Christian experience of faith we have no organ which can give us a view of Jesus's resurrection. But conversely: without the personal resurrection of Jesus there can be no Christian experience of Easter (IR, p. 79).

Quite obviously, a philosophical presupposition asserting the interdependence of subject and object is operative in Schillebeeckx's theological interpretation of Jesus' resurrection and appearances.

Three other points stand out in Schillebeeckx's interpretation of resurrection faith. First, faith in the resurrection is taken to be an initial evaluation of Jesus' life and death and a recognition of the essential importance of Jesus' praxis and proclamation of God's kingdom. Second, it is a manifestation of something already present during Jesus' life, namely, his intimate communion with the living God. Thirdly, resurrection faith expresses a recognition of a divine judgement on what humans did to Jesus (III, pp. 129–30).

SCHILLEBEECKX'S RESPONSE TO LESSING

In view of the points made above concerning Jesus' praxis in favour of the outcast, it now becomes possible to consider Schillebeeckx's rejoinder to Gotthold Lessing.

All three books in Schillebeeckx's Christological trilogy seek to expound the sense of Christian faith's claim that Jesus is universally significant for all peoples at all times. Otherwise stated, in

Schillebeeckx's view, a historical particularity, Jesus of Nazareth, can still be said to have a universally applicable importance. And yet, to say that Jesus is important for all people as a revelation of a divinely wrought salvation is an affirmation of faith, not an unambiguous statement of a universally observable fact. Recognizing that since the Enlightenment, people of the modern world are critically-minded (I, p. 114), Schillebeeckx attempts to take issue in his trilogy with a particular, post-Enlightenment form of critical, rationalist thought, exemplified by Lessing, and according to which the idea that universal salvation can be mediated by a historical particularity is regarded as a pre-critical naïvety. Acknowledging, full well, that a historical particularity cannot be canonized into a general principle, Schillebeeckx advances what he calls the sound epistemological principle of 'universality through a historically particular intermediary' (I, p. 592).

We arrive, then, at a conclusion of utmost significance. For Schillebeeckx, *Christian faith is universal because it is partisan.* Because it is bent on humanizing humanity by liberating the socially oppressed, it includes within the ambit of its concern sections of society excluded by reigning policies or ideologies: 'Because of its universality, which does not exclude anyone, Christian love, seen in social and political terms, is in practice partisan — otherwise it is not universal!' (III, p. 178).

While he does not say so in so many words, I would explain Schillebeeckx's response to Lessing in the following way. Over and against Lessing's disclaimer that universality can be mediated in a historical particularity, Schillebeeckx proffers the view that universality can be mediated through particularity in two main ways. The first concerns the *subject* of a praxis of liberation. The second has to do with the *interest* of a praxis. To explain: if the subject of an emancipatory praxis is the social outcast, then universality comes into play because the suffering of the outcast is a universal human phenomenon. And secondly, if the interest of a praxis is to promote justice, then universality is once more involved, because justice is, philosophically speaking, a universal. By an appeal to the interest and subject of praxis, therefore, Schillebeeckx makes an effective response to Lessing's type of rationalism.

In my opinion, however, Schillebeeckx fails to respond adequately to Lessing, and this for two reasons. First, Schillebeeckx describes the uniqueness of Jesus in terms of the latter's intimate consciousness of being constituted in a unique relation to God, as Son to Father (III, pp. 118–19). A rationalist in the line of Lessing, however, could claim that Jesus was a self-deluded megalomaniac. Secondly, Schillebeeckx asserts that part of an individual's identity stems from his or her influence in subsequent history (I, p. 19). Jesus is universally relevant, one supposes, because a church grew up in his wake. Once again, though, a rationalist sceptic could point out that many figures in history have had legions of followers. Yet their lives and conduct need not be of perduring significance for all people at all times.

CONCLUSION

To draw this chapter to a close I should like to stress once again that Schillebeeckx's Christology is characterized by a continually present overriding interest, and an altered manner of thinking about the interest. His governing Christological aim or interest is to explain in what sense Jesus is the manifestation of a universal salvation stemming from God. In his early Christology he explained Jesus' uniqueness and mediation of universality by relying on the definition of Chalcedon: Jesus saves because he is a God–man. In the later Christology, however, the universality of divine salvation is mediated through Jesus' praxis aimed at emancipating the poor, and in the praxis of those who seek to emulate Jesus.

One reason why Schillebeeckx may be regarded as an outstanding Christian thinker is that his Christological trilogy argues that all talk of Christian identity and universal significance needs to consider the present and the future. It is not sufficient to express the meaning of faith by ransacking the New Testament for texts testifying to Christ's unimpeachable integrity, or to Christianity's perennial worth. What Jesus said and did, and what Christian faith means, remains to be demonstrated partially in the behaviour of contemporary Christians; it depends to some extent on their praxis. And while human history continues, there can be no precipitous talk of knowledge of universal truth or meaning, because the plenitude of meaning includes a future which has not yet been realized. One can practically anticipate meaning, therefore, in actions designed to shape a more humane future. All of which is captured in Schillebeeckx's lapidary phrase: 'Jesus's light burns in this world only with the oil of our lives' (II, p. 846).

Notes

1 GM, p. 11. Schillebeeckx also talks about children and the crib in his article 'God in menselijkheid', *Tijdschrift voor Geestelijk Leven* 13 (1957), pp. 697–710 (pp. 697–8).

2 GM, p. 18. This text is actually the opening paragraph of Schillebeeckx's inaugural lecture in Nijmegen.

3 See Gregory of Nyssa, *Commentary on the Song of Songs*, Homily 1 (ch. 1, v. 3).

4 See Edward Schillebeeckx, 'Ik geloof in Jezus van Nazareth', *Tijdschrift voor Geestelijk Leven* 35 (1979), pp. 451–73 (pp. 452–3), from which the title of this chapter is taken; and III, p. 179, for the quotation just cited.

5 See Vincent A. McCarthy, *Quest for a Philosophical Jesus: Christianity and Philosophy in Rousseau, Kant, Hegel, and Schelling* (Macon, GA: Mercer University Press, 1986), p. xi; and Michael J. Buckley, *At the Origins of Modern Atheism* (New Haven and London: Yale University Press, 1987), pp. 38–41.

6 Schillebeeckx, 'Catholic life in the United States', *Worship* 42 (1968), pp. 134–49 (p. 137).

7 See SC, p. 60; and I, p. 29.

8   Consult John E. Thiel, *Imagination and Authority: Theological Authorship in the Modern Tradition* (Minneapolis: Fortress Press, 1991), pp. 2–8.

9   Gotthold Lessing, 'On the proof of the Spirit and of power' in *Lessing's Theological Writings*, sel. and trans. Henry Chadwick (London: A. & C. Black, 1956/Stanford, CA: Stanford University Press, 1957), pp. 51–6 (pp. 55 and 53). For a sustained and nuanced analysis of the ugly-ditch imagery in Lessing, see Gordon E. Michalson, *Lessing's 'Ugly Ditch': A Study of Theology and History* (University Park and London: Pennsylvania State University Press, 1985), esp. pp. 1–21. Michalson clarifies that Lessing had three ditches in mind, not one.

10 See Edward Schillebeeckx, *Christologia* (mimeographed notes; Stichting Edward Schillebeeckx: Katholieke Universiteit Nijmegen, undated, but before 1957), 369pp. (pp. II, 101–3); and GNM, p. 19, where the importance of Aquinas's text for Schillebeeckx is brought to light.

11 See A. Hulsbosch, 'Jezus Christus, gekend als mens, beleden als Zoon Gods', *Tijdschrift voor Theologie* 6 (1966), pp. 250–73.

12 See Edward Schillebeeckx, 'Persoonlijke openbaringsgestalte van de Vader', *Tijdschrift voor Theologie* 6 (1966), pp. 274–88 (pp. 278–83).

13 See Edward Schillebeeckx, 'De levensweg van Jezus, beleden als de Christus' in Marcel Messing (ed.), *Religie als Levende Ervaring* (Assen/Maastricht: Van Gorcum, 1988), pp. 136–49.

14 Edward Schillebeeckx, 'De toegang tot Jezus van Nazareth', *Tijdschrift voor Theologie* 12 (1972), pp. 28–60.

15 Schillebeeckx explains his method in SC, pp. 52–4.

16 Edward Schillebeeckx, 'Critical theories and Christian political commitment', *Concilium* 84 (1974), pp. 48–61 (p. 50). The original Dutch version appeared in 1973.

17 See, for instance, the work of Sean Freyne, *Galilee, Jesus and the Gospels: Literary Approaches and Historical Investigations* (Philadelphia: Fortress Press, 1988).

7

Knowing God negatively

In 1600, the Italian Dominican friar Giordano Bruno was burnt at the stake as a heretic in Rome. He lost his life because his philosophical and cosmological ideas were judged at the time to be incompatible with Christian faith. In 1889, the year Nietzsche became insane and a year before he died, and one hundred years after the French Revolution, a statue dedicated to Bruno was erected in Rome, much to the annoyance of the incumbent Pope, Leo XIII. In 1989, almost four hundred years after Bruno's death, a volume of the French journal *Lignes* was published in Paris and dedicated to the memory of both Bruno and Nietzsche. The volume bore the title 'In Praise of Irreligion'. Its editorial lamented the return or recrudescence of religion in the world over the past fifteen years, and expressed the volume's aim to affirm and fortify the right of an individual not to believe, and to laugh and swear against gods.[1]

The freedom to forswear religious belief publicly, and to lampoon Christian faith with impunity, is a relatively recent phenomenon in European history. While forms of non-belief are well recorded in ancient philosophical schools between, let us say, 300 BCE and 450 CE, once Christianity gained imperial favour in the fourth century, and went on to exercise hegemonic control over much of Europe, at least in the opinion of one author, 'it turned upon other religions and unsympathetic philosophies, and even upon variations of its own doctrines, with an ideological ferocity that was previously unknown in the world'.[2] Even so, after the seventeenth-century wars of religion, and following the collapse of traditional social order in Europe in the eighteenth century, renunciations of Christianity became more public and widespread, thus preparing the way for the development of widespread and state atheism in more modern times. Indeed, especially since the eighteenth century, and following the French, American, Industrial and Scientific Revolutions, classical Catholic and Protestant theologies have had 'to

120

fight for life against wave after wave of criticism from both inside and outside organized Christianity'.[3]

In this light, one of the more remarkable aspects of Edward Schillebeeckx's theology is the unmistakable, unswerving, and seemingly foolhardy confidence with which he argues, in full view of full-blown atheism and secularization, that God can be known by human beings. He quite readily admits, to use his own words, that the 'word "God" caresses man's lips far less now than it did in the past' (WC, p. 78). And yet he wilfully espouses that: 'Never before in history has God's presence in the world been so intimate and so tangibly real as now, in our own time, yet we do nothing but proclaim his absence everywhere . . .' (WC, p. 78). Far from being intimidated by the arguments of unbelief and attempts to debunk Christianity, Schillebeeckx proclaims, somewhat against the grain, that 'no matter in what circumstances we find ourselves, whether through blind chance, determinism or our own fault, there is no situation in which God cannot come near to us and in which we would not be able to find him' (III, p. 11).

Quite apart from persisting in professing faith in God, Schillebeeckx explains the genesis of faith with reference to exactly the same human experience relied upon by some atheists to discount belief. The experience I have in mind is none other than contingency. As noted above, Schillebeeckx is partial to the view that both believers and non-believers share the common experience of being constrained by their finiteness and contingency. He concludes, however, that this experience can be interpreted contrastively. With Sartre, to take his favourite test case, there is nothing apart from contingency: there is no other side to finiteness, as it were. Contrariwise, in Schillebeeckx's terms, contingency can be interpreted as the other side of the absolute gratuitous presence of God. Whereas for Sartre contingency is all-that-is and points to emptiness, for Schillebeeckx it is merely a limitation that refers to its source, the plenitude of God.

In this chapter I want to highlight further Schillebeeckx's eminence as a Christian thinker and shed additional light on the distinctiveness of his thought by attending to the manner in which he speaks about human cognitional contact with God. We have noted previously that he is a philosophically informed theologian. More than that, his philosophical interests have been especially governed by questions concerning knowledge. There is no philosophical issue more central to his theological project than the matter of human knowledge of God or, in other words, the issue of knowledge of universality by particularity. It is important to consider his clarification of this matter because his approach sets him apart from other major twentieth-century Roman Catholic theologians such as Hans Küng and Karl Rahner. While Küng is inclined to find God in aesthetics, to generalize, Schillebeeckx points to experiences of suffering as a privileged terrain in which it becomes possible to perceive what faith in God might mean. And whereas Karl Rahner analyses human subjectivity as a dynamic reference to God, Schillebeeckx insists that the objective reality of God itself is the source of faith in that it draws a believer's subjectivity towards itself (see GM, p. 25). In these terms human cognitive intersubjectivity with God is not regarded as a self-achievement. Rahner's works certainly do not suggest that, but the difference here is a matter of emphasis. Rahner has an anthropological starting point for talking about faith and he emphasizes the importance of human subjectivity. Schillebeeckx draws attention to a divine creation in which human subjects inhere in God: 'We dwell in God as in our own house' (RT2, p. 109).[4]

In seeking to indicate Schillebeeckx's pre-eminence as a Christian thinker in the specific context of his discussions of religious knowledge, that is, human knowledge of God, two significant points need to be made. First, his entire manner of speaking about religious knowledge is, as we shall see, profoundly traditional. And second, in the context of a new, distinctively twentieth-century form of theologizing, namely, liberation theology, he has been able to transpose an ancient, traditional way of speaking about religious knowledge into contemporary theological and philosophical categories. All of which is to highlight, yet again, that his theological disquisitions are characterized by continuity and discontinuity. Throughout his career he has been persistently preoccupied by the question of religious knowledge and he has always argued that faith is a form of knowledge through which God can be known. And yet, even while undeviatingly holding the issue of religious knowledge firmly in view throughout his writings, he has certainly altered the way he has explained believers' knowledge of God.

The nature of this alteration needs to be brought home. In his early work he maintained, for example, that an individual encounters and knows God most of all in the context of ecclesiastical sacraments (see WC, p. 160, and CS, p. 212). In his later work, he observes strongly that an individual encounters God in association with other people, mutually engaged in a struggle to humanize the world. There is no verb more significant in Schillebeeckx's vocabulary than the infinitive 'to humanize': it is in practically striving to humanize or ameliorate dehumanized and subhuman conditions of living that a believer finds a privileged access to knowledge of God (see JWC, pp. 63–4). Consequently, in Schillebeeckx's later theology, the most important question which arises with regard to belief in God is this: 'Which side do you choose in the struggle between good and evil, between oppressors and oppressed?' (III, p. 7). And again:

Anyone who begins to speak of God too early in this context [of the history of human liberation] arouses the suspicion of talking about an antiquated image of God, about the God of a former picture of the world and society, the God of a handful of rich people, to the detriment of the oppressed and those who have to live on the periphery of society. The real deciding factor is: are we as Christians (perhaps in the whole of our historically and socially privileged situation) in solidarity with the oppressed and the isolated, or are we on the side of the powerful and the oppressors? In the preferential love of men and women for the poor there is an implicit confirmation of what Christians call God's free being: unconditional love; love without a condition. (Ibid.)

One notices immediately that Schillebeeckx's later discussion of God and human contact with the divine is not tied to an explicitly intellectual and formally speculative exercise. The distinctiveness of his religious epistemology resides primarily in two factors. First, it does not regard either knowledge as such, or religious knowledge in particular, as reducible purely to explicit conceptuality. In this, the style of Schillebeeckx's approach finds ample testimony in the work of professional philosophers.[5] Second, his religious epistemology is tied to the history of a particular individual — Jesus of Nazareth. To clarify in his own words:

talk about God can, as such, never be empirical or purely descriptive. The real context within which the Christian speaks about God, then, is that of the life, death and resurrection of the man Jesus, acknowledged to be the Christ, the one who is the living prototype of and determines the ultimate meaning of our human life and history. . . . (UF, p. 86)

Hans Küng has explicitly noted that whereas 'in Schillebeeckx the problem of God is addressed primarily in the field of Christology, in my case it is given a philosophical–theological treatment against the whole horizon of the modern period in a separate volume'.[6] The two factors just mentioned explain why Schillebeeckx ripostes against disavowals of Christianity based on purely abstract, logical or theoretical perspectives.

CONSCIOUS IGNORANCE OF GOD

It is quite difficult to understand Schillebeeckx's explanations of religious knowledge, or to unravel what could be called in a more technical fashion his epistemology of religious experience, even if only because his writings elaborate knowledge of God in the diverse manners mentioned above. I shall now consider these manners separately, and then illustrate how they actually amount to suggesting very much the same thing.

To begin with, let us consider Schillebeeckx's early explanations of the cognitivity of religious faith, that is, his elaborations falling between the mid-1940s and the mid-1960s. The first point to be made here is that, for Schillebeeckx, faith is a genuine form of knowledge. Like any other type of cognition, it has a bipartite structure in that it involves two indissociable elements. One is represented by concepts; the other is non-conceptual. In this view knowledge is realized in an interplay between the two indivisible elements. According to Schillebeeckx's early works, concepts in themselves do not describe or contact God's reality: every concept of God is godless because it denies God's transcendence. On a purely conceptual level, therefore, human beings are said to be ignorant of God. To justify cognitive contact with God, therefore, Schillebeeckx hypothesizes that a non-conceptual though strictly noetic (knowledge-value) feature of knowledge has an objective reference, or points, towards God's reality. In short, his entire early manner of speaking about religious knowledge is captured in his paradoxical assertion that knowledge of God is realized in a *conscious ignorance*.[7]

When discussing Schillebeeckx's disquisitions on religious knowledge it is important to note that he is able to express subtleties in Dutch which escape the English language. English uses the one verb, 'to know', to designate types of knowledge as varied as the empirical and the mystical. Dutch, however, has two different verbs signifying 'to know': *kennen* and *weten*. *Kennen* is used in association with persons; it means to know some*one*. Its cognate noun, *kenbaarheid*, designates 'recognizability'. *Weten*, however, means to know an item of data or a fact. It is normally used in the context of knowing some*thing*. When speaking of knowledge of God, Schillebeeckx uses forms of both verbs. He says that human beings can enjoy a positive knowledge of God in conscious ignorance ('een positieve kennis in bewuste onwetendheid').[8] The ignorance mentioned rests on the level of empirical, scientific, or conceptual knowledge (*onwetendheid*). The positive knowledge is linked to a cognition between persons (*kennis*).

THE EPISTEMOLOGICAL RESEARCHES OF LOUVAIN

The mainstay, then, of Schillebeeckx's early explanations of religious knowledge was his hypothesis that knowledge is simultaneously conceptual and non-conceptual. It would be more accurate to say that his hypothesis was actually Dominic De Petter's, since the latter made a similar distinction within the field of epistemology while teaching in Louvain. Schillebeeckx took over De Petter's distinction and applied it directly in a theological context to the question of human knowledge of God.

The early work of both Karl Rahner and Edward Schillebeeckx needs to be considered in the light of the philosophy of a Belgian Jesuit, Joseph Maréchal. During World War I, Maréchal began to publish a five-volume work on metaphysics. Rahner avidly read the fifth volume and found there a theory concerning the dynamism of the human spirit.[9] Maréchal had sought to analyse knowledge by developing, among other matters, epistemological axioms of classical Thomism. It is something of a commonplace to observe that Descartes brought epistemology to a place of central importance in Western philosophy. It should not be forgotten, however, that questions concerning knowledge were very much at the centre of mediaeval theological and philosophical reflection.[10] Thomas Aquinas, as a clear case in point, had a good deal to say about knowledge in the first part of his *Summa Theologiae*, and in the second book of his *Summa Contra Gentiles*. Aquinas, like Aristotle, maintained that the intellectual soul or mind is, in the cognitional process, *initially* like a blank tablet (*tabula rasa*) on which nothing is impressed.[11] For Thomas, knowledge originates in a knower's sensate perception of actually existing beings: knowledge results from a collaboration between external and internal senses and their grasp of sensible, particular and material things, and the dynamic interplay between active and passive intellects which, commencing with a process of abstraction, culminates in the formation of an immaterial and universal concept, through which the essence or nature instantiated in the particular is understood. This is not the place to explain further Thomas's quite intricate understanding of cognitional processes. Suffice it to emphasize, though, that Maréchal built on Thomas's work in the explicit light of Descartes and Kant, after whom the idea that the mind is an active contributor in the workings of knowledge became a prominent part of the common patrimony of a good deal of modern philosophy.[12] Maréchal, in short, sought to reinterpret St Thomas in dialogue with Kantian epistemology.

The all-important feature of Maréchal's analysis of religious knowledge is this: in denying that knowledge is purely conceptual or notional, he assumed that the basis of knowledge (of God) resides in a non-noetic, concept-transcending dynamism of the human spirit.

We need not delay with a detailed examination of Maréchal's epistemology. Suffice it to record here that De Petter elaborated a theory of knowledge opposed to Maréchal's. While both agreed that knowledge is bipartite with conceptual and non-conceptual polarities, De Petter insisted that the non-conceptual element is still strictly noetic or intellectual, and not something which is extra-intellectual or volitional.

De Petter published his response to Maréchal in 1939 with an article entitled 'Implicit intuition'.[13] Over and against Maréchal's idea that cognitive contact with reality is located in a volitional dynamism of a knowing subject, De Petter advanced the theory that an individual's intellect involves an intuition-moment which makes contact with extra-mental reality. More than that, he contended that the intuitive factor establishes a cognitive awareness of the *total* meaning of reality.

SCHILLEBEECKX'S 'CLEAR BREAK' WITH DE PETTER

Schillebeeckx relied on De Petter's epistemology to expound the cognitivity of Christian faith until the mid-1960s. Then his philosophical thinking transformed. For the purposes of grasping what was involved in Schillebeeckx's philosophical evolution in the 1960s, no text is more tantalizingly enigmatic than a passage that appears towards the end of his book *Jesus: An Experiment in Christology*. In the fourth part of the book, and in the context of discussing the question of ultimate meaning and particular experiences of meaning, Schillebeeckx spoke of having long ago realized that to assert that theses of faith need to be tested in the realm of historical experiences 'entails a clear break with the "implicit intuition" of meaning-totality maintained by classical philosophy like that of D. de Petter, L. Lavelle and the French *philosophes de l'Esprit'* (I, p. 618). We should note parenthetically that De Petter's name is rendered here as 'de Petter' following Dutch custom, rather than in the Flemish idiom of 'De Petter'. In any event, this passage is highly enigmatic for a number of reasons. First, in its original Dutch version Schillebeeckx describes the philosophy he is breaking with as *classicale*. This is most probably a slip on his part for the normal Dutch equivalent of the English 'classical' is *klassiek*. In the second instance, he describes as classical (if this is what he means by *classicale*) De Petter, Lavelle, and the French philosophers of the spirit. What is strange about this encompassing designation is that De Petter's philosophy is not like Lavelle's. And even if it were, what is to be made of the fact that De Petter was dismissed from his responsibilities as Regent of Studies in the Dominican House of Studies in Louvain in 1942, precisely because he was not considered as classical on account of his importation of Kantian epistemology into his reinterpretation of Aquinas's work?

So: the cryptic, though all-important remark about a clear break with De Petter's theory of implicit intuition of a totality of meaning is not adequately clarified in the first book on Jesus. For a clearer elaboration of what the remark implies, we need to delve into archival material. On 4 December 1968, Schillebeeckx gave an informal exposition of his thought to Dominican students in the Order's House of Studies in Nijmegen. The talk he gave was recorded and a transcript of his comments was produced. The transcript helps to understand why Schillebeeckx altered his way of elaborating religious knowledge. At the commencement of his encounter with the students he was asked a direct question: 'Do you still believe in the epistemology, in the gnoseology of Father De Petter or not?'[14] Revealingly, Schillebeeckx responded by saying that De Petter's epistemology no longer enjoyed any importance in his thought at that time. He went on to qualify his stance, however, by stating that he wished to retain De Petter's metaphysical-ontological thought, but to give it an existential basis. The key comment to retain in this light is the remark concerning an existential basis. In the end, Schillebeeckx's quibble with De Petter's philosophy was that it was idealistically prejudiced, which is to say, that it betrayed an exaggerated interest in speculation over and against things in themselves (transcript, p. 1). All of the major intellectual currents that surface in Schillebeeckx's writings, currents such as existentialism and phenomenology and Critical Theory, initially emerged against the background of a much broader movement of modern philosophical reflection away from entertaining abstractions to examining more concrete and social matters (see RT2, p. 5).

Schillebeeckx's philosophical turnabout, therefore, was an exchange of an aprioristic epistemology for an *a posteriori* theory of knowledge. Expressed more plainly, after the mid-1960s, for reasons outlined in a previous chapter, he assumed that knowledge of reality arises in the first place in the context of action or praxis, and in a secondary step, becomes explicitly accounted for in a process of speculation.

And so: Schillebeeckx's early explanation of religious knowledge was to a very large extent an unashamedly theoretical construct. His later explanation counterbalanced a theoretical bent by attempting, as he indicated in 1968, to endow it with what he called an existential basis.

ETHICS, POLITICS AND MYSTICISM

The reader of Schillebeeckx's later works would have every reason to feel confused regarding the way in which he began to speak about knowledge of God after his philosophical switch. For, on the one hand, he asserts latterly that God is accessible above all in an ethical praxis. On the other hand, he insists that cognitive contact with God is achieved in virtue of a mystical dimension of faith. So which is it: is God met and known in a praxis seeking justice, or in a mystical experience?

The situation we have with Schillebeeckx's later explanations of religious knowledge can be untangled as follows. In his works since the mid-1960s he explains God's accessibility to human knowledge by emphasizing the multidimensionality of Christian faith. He does not regard faith as some kind of monochrome state of inner reflection. On the contrary, he considers it as an amalgam of distinct elements which may be described as interpersonal, ecological, sociopolitical, and mystical (JWC, p. 65). The key elements to underscore here are the mystical and political polarities. By mysticism, he means 'an intensive form of experience of God or love of God' (JWC, pp. 71–2). By politics, as we observed elsewhere (see p. 111), he means 'an intensive form of social commitment' (JWC, p. 72).

The point to bear in mind now is that Schillebeeckx speaks about ethics so as to link the political and mystical dimensions of faith. By ethics he intends nothing less than an activity bent on humanizing human existence, if the phrase be allowed (see III, pp. 91–2). Through an ethical commitment to improve social conditions by way of a praxis seeking justice, it becomes possible, so the argument evolves, to experience something of God's reality.

NEGATIVE CONTRAST EXPERIENCES

We come now to yet another vital category attending on Schillebeeckx's later explanations of religious knowledge: the notion of a negative contrast experience. Within his more recent work, an ethical praxis bent on humanizing unjust situations becomes the condition for a cognitive contact with God that is said to blossom in a mystical aspect of faith. Be that as it may, the ethical praxis in question stems itself from the broader context of what Schillebeeckx calls a negative contrast experience. If a sacrament constituted the apex of religious experience in his initial publications, then negative experiences of contrast are elevated to epistemological paramountcy in his later works: 'they form a basic human experience which as such I regard as being a pre-religious and thus a basic experience accessible to all human beings, namely that of a "no" to the world as it is' (III, p. 5).

What, then, in more detail, is a negative contrast experience that is supposed to form a seed-bed for a cognitive experience of God? In the mid-1960s, Schillebeeckx diagnosed religion's functional loss in secularized societies wherein Christianity and belief in God apparently no longer functioned as substitutes for everything that appeared inexplicable in terms of science and reason (see GFM, pp. 174–5). He set out to search for a new way in which Christian faith could function in secularized settings and he eventually described this function as a critical negativity, by which he meant, not an irascible criticism of all things modern, but a *positive power* to humanize the world (GFM, pp. 191 and 199).

By speaking of faith's social function in terms of a critical negativity, Schillebeeckx certainly implied an element of forceful social critique. But the critical negativity he had in mind involved a positive element tied to a negative one. The negative was envisaged as a criticism of social predicaments that belittle human beings. The positive element is linked to something that has not yet been brought about, to wit, a more human situation imagined, hoped for, and sought after in the future. Because the positive element of faith's critical negativity is tied to an unrealized future, it cannot be defined explicitly and positively. It can only be partially perceived in a negative way. To clarify what is implied in such a negative manner, Schillebeeckx brings the notion of negative contrast experiences into play.

It is of the utmost importance to observe that his idea of a negative contrast experience is not an experience simply of a negative thing, such as suffering. It is actually a double-edged experience linked to the notion of prophecy. A negative contrast experience (in Schillebeeckx's account) has both a negative and a positive face. To begin with, it is an experience of the disordered nature of human existence and of suffering (III, p. 5). However and happily, a sense of indignation eventually emerges from within such a negative experience: the very experience of debilitating suffering *contrasts* with a more worthy and human situation envisaged in the midst of suffering; and the perception of contrast triggers a sense of indignation which refuses to submit to the inanity of suffering. The sense of indignation is associated with an incipient awareness of hope which prompts a prophetic protest against the causes of suffering.

And so, a negative contrast experience militates against what should not be, on the basis of a hope in what should be.[15]

FROM CONCEPTUAL TO PRACTICAL APOPHATISM

To revert to Schillebeeckx's early writings, it seems clear that at the very heart of their explanations of religious knowledge stands a notion of negativity: God is not known directly through concepts, but indirectly through analogy; concepts refer to God, but cognitive contact with divinity is achievable in a non-conceptual component of knowledge. Thus commented upon, Schillebeeckx is classifiable as a profoundly traditional theologian. Traditional, that is, in that he stands in a long line of theological reflection which is technically called apophatic. 'Apophatic' is simply another way of saying 'negative'. The basic idea behind apophatism is that we can only really say what God is not. All our positive descriptions of, and names for, God—kataphatic theology—are merely human constructions that in no way capture what is distinctly *of God*. Apophatic theologies insist that all human images and doctrines of the divine are human formulations which cannot be regarded as notions emanating from God. While the reality of God is certainly not a human product, concepts referring to God inescapably are. Classic instances of apophatic theologies are found, to be selective, in Augustine, Pseudo-Dionysius the Areopagite and Thomas Aquinas. What Schillebeeckx calls a conscious ignorance in relation to religious knowledge, St Augustine labelled as a 'learned ignorance'. To quote the saint: 'We cannot know God as God is, indeed we do not know God; there is in us what I might call a kind of "learned ignorance"—learned because it is instructed by the Holy Spirit, who helps our weakness'.[16]

Now, the really striking characteristic of Schillebeeckx's later explanation of religious knowledge is that it betrays the same bipartite structure as his early work. Both his initial and latter-day writings speak of God's accessibility to human beings in the context of an interplay between indissociable positive and negative elements. In the early works, the positive factor, implicit intuition, or the non-conceptual aspect of knowledge, sustains the negative feature of conceptuality, passing through it, so to speak, to refer to God. In these terms, God is known negatively only by way of a conceptual analogy. In the later writings, however, the implicit intuition is transposed into the notion of a positive hope that arises in suffering, and the negativity of conceptuality assumes the form of the negativity inherent in experiential suffering. In both the early and later works the actual cognitive contact with God is achieved in an implicit, inexpressible dimension of faith. In Schillebeeckx's own words: 'mysticism in the more special sense is an intense form of experience of this cognitive element in faith which binds us with God' (JWC, p. 66).

In my opinion, Schillebeeckx is an outstanding Christian thinker, because he has been able to transfigure a classical theological tradition of conceptual apophatism into a late twentieth-century practical apophatism. This point requires explanation.

Aquinas had worked under the assumption that Pseudo-Dionysius the Areopagite was a contemporary of St Paul of Tarsus and hence a member of the first Christian generation. Subsequent scholarship has shown that the Dionysius quoted by St Thomas, now referred to as Pseudo-Dionysius, actually wrote towards the beginning of the sixth Christian century, or thereabouts. In any case, the conclusion to retain is that Pseudo-Dionysius's negative theology left its mark on Aquinas. Both Schillebeeckx's early and later writings refer to a threefold way in which classical apophaticism, as typified by Aquinas, sought to say something positive about God (see RT2, pp. 162–78; and III, pp. 76–7).

St Thomas taught that creatures cannot know incorporeal things or substances except negatively, through an analogy with corporeal realities.[17] But if all that believers can say of God is what God is not, then language about God can appear vacuous and ineffectual because it is unable to affirm anything positively of God. Traditional apophatic theologies attempted to state something positive concerning God by way of a threefold operation called the *via triplex*, or the three ways. This manner of speaking about God involved the successive phases of affirmation (*via affirmativa*), negation (*via negativa*), and eminence (*via eminentiae*). With the first step believers apply concepts of faith, such as names and images, to God. They say, for example, that God is Good, or a Father, or again, in Schillebeeckx's case, a Pure Positivity. On closer inspection, though, it soon becomes evident that these positive predicates of God have a creaturely provenance and express more about their users than their referent. God is good, so the argument then turns, but not in the way human beings are said to be good. And so, immediately on having taken the step of the affirmative way, it is incumbent upon the believer to negate that step through a way of negation which insists that positive conceptual affirmations about God are ineffectual. Yet this negation of affirmation is itself negated in a third manoeuvre, the way of eminence, which recognizes that God transcends human conceptuality, though in a supereminently divine fashion. In the third step, it is asserted that God is at least everything imagined in human concepts, although in an incomparably surpassing divine mode.

Classically conceived, in the *via triplex* with its three steps of assertion, negation, and reassertion in a supereminent mode, the really axial move is negation: it is this which safeguards, so to say, God's transcendence. A statement declaring, for example, that God is good as a human being is good, posits a similarity between God and humanity. Yet God is neither finite nor hidebound by spatio-temporality. Therefore, it becomes necessary to advert to the dissimilarity between God's goodness and human goodness; it is necessary to negate or purify the concept of goodness of its experienced finiteness before it can be applied analogously to God.

With a determinative difference, Schillebeeckx rehearses the traditional conceptual *via triplex* in the third part of his Christological trilogy (III, pp. 76–7). The pivotal difference is this: the knowledge of the *via eminentiae* is no longer regarded as the outgrowth of a *conceptual via negativa*, but of a *practical* or *experiential* one:

> we do not learn to know the *via eminentiae* beyond affirmation and negation in and through a conceptual interplay of thought, but in and from the history of solidarity, justice and love made by men and women in a world of egotism, injustice and lovelessness. (III, p. 77)

What this statement belies is, on the one hand, its author's resolute acknowledgement of liberation theology's adversarial advocacy of the poor, and, on the other, a Christian variation of Theodor Adorno's Western Marxist *via negativa*. Schillebeeckx's concept of Christian faith's social function as a critical negativity was inspired by Adorno's work *Negative Dialectics*. He acknowledges as much in his book *God the Future of Man* (p. 205, n. 8). Nevertheless, while Adorno's negative dialectics, or *via negativa*, espoused a pure negativity and did not put forward anything positive,[18] Schillebeeckx's critical negativity is fired by a hope in a more humane existence that is conceived as the outgrowth of a practical and prophetic resistance to suffering.

Clearly, the apophatism of classical Christian theology after Pseudo-Dionysius rests on a theoretical negativity issuing from a conceptual, linguistic analogy. In other words, the negation incurred in speaking about God involves a negation on an analogical level of concepts. After Schillebeeckx's philosophical turnabout, when he came to speak much more about praxis, he effectively translated the conceptual negativity of his earlier discussions of how God is known to a practical negativity: God is found and known above all in the midst of actions that seek to surmount and suppress suffering. And this is precisely why Schillebeeckx once felt confident to state that never before in human history has God's presence been so tangibly real as now. That statement was made in 1966, looking back at a Europe pillaged by world wars. After the wars, Schillebeeckx spoke of an augmentation of human solidarity. Service to others, so he said,

> is becoming a fundamental project in life and an effective force. Surely this is precisely what is happening in our own time—it is the central event of grace in post-war world history. God has consequently come infinitely more close to us now than he was in the past. (WC, p. 78)

To conclude, Schillebeeckx's mature theology makes much of the idea that God cannot be known apart from human, social relationships, and in so doing it echoes Habermas's stance that if one has knowledge of anything at all, one must have intersubjectivity.[19] In his later works, Schillebeeckx also explicitly endorses Lévinas's maxim that no knowledge of God can be attained apart from social relationships.[20] And yet, even though his publications of the last two and a half decades chime and abound with the terminology of Habermasian Critical Theory and Lévinas's ethics, his latter-day discourses on knowing God negatively, discourses that tell of a mystical faith-moment welded to an ethical praxis of justice arising from the midst of a negative contrast experience, do not constitute an entirely novel viewpoint. His latter-day discourses certainly amount to a philosophical mouthful. In the long run, however, they are not very far removed from the time-honoured Christian hymnic declaration, 'Ubi caritas et amor, Deus ibi est'— 'Where there is charity and love, there also is God.'

Notes

1 See Michel Surya, 'Editorial', *Lignes* 6: *Eloge de l'Irréligion* (1989), pp. 8–10.
2 J. C. A. Gaskin (ed.), 'Introduction' in *Varieties of Unbelief: Epicurus to Sartre* (New York and London: Macmillan, 1989), pp. 1–16 (p. 5).
3 John H. S. Kent, *The End of the Line?: The Development of Christian Theology in the Last Two Centuries* (London: SCM, 1982), p. 1.
4 For illustrations of points made in this paragraph, consult Hans Küng, 'Rediscovering God', *Concilium* (1990/1; London: SCM, 1990), pp. 86–102; and Karl Rahner, *Foundations of Christian Faith: An Introduction to the Idea of Christianity* (London: Darton, Longman & Todd, 1978), pp. 1–137.
5 See, to give just one example, William P. Alston, *Perceiving God: The Epistemology of Religious Experience* (Ithaca and London: Cornell University Press, 1991), esp. pp. 1–8.
6 Hans Küng, *Theology for the Third Millennium: An Ecumenical View* (New York: Doubleday, 1988), p. 107. The separate volume Küng refers to here is his book *Existiert Gott?* (Munich: Piper Verlag, 1978), Eng. trans. *Does God Exist?: An Answer for Today* (New York: Doubleday/London: Collins, 1980).
7 For Schillebeeckx's early approach to religious knowledge see RT1, pp. 133–4; RT2, pp. 30–75 and 155–206; and GM, pp. 292–8.
8 Edward Schillebeeckx, 'Evangelische zuiverhuid en menselijke waarachtigheid', *Tijdschrift voor Theologie* 3 (1963), pp. 283–326 (p. 297).
9 See Karl Rahner, *Faith in a Wintry Season: Conversations and Interviews with Karl Rahner in the Last Years of His Life* (New York: Crossroad, 1990), pp. 42–7.
10 See Alexander Broadie, *Notion and Object: Aspects of Late Medieval Epistemology* (Oxford: Clarendon Press, 1989), p. 1.
11 See Aquinas's *Summa Theologiae*, Ia, q. 79, a. 2.
12 Consult Jaakko Hintikka, *Knowledge and the Known: Historical Perspectives in Epistemology* (Dordrecht, Boston, and London: Kluwer Academic Publishers, 1991), esp. p. 127.
13 D. M. De Petter, 'Impliciete Intuïtie', *Tijdschrift voor Philosophie* 1 (1939), pp. 84–105.
14 Edward Schillebeeckx, *Voor O.P. Studium Albertinum* (typed transcript, '4. XII. 1968'; Stichting Edward Schillebeeckx: Katholieke Universiteit Nijmegen, 1968), 7pp. (p. 1).

15 See Edward Schillebeeckx, 'Theologische draagwijdte van het magisteriële spreken over sociaal-politieke kwesties', *Concilium* 4 (1968), pp. 21–40 (pp. 33–4).

16 Augustine, *Epistulae*, epist. 139.14.27–15.28; trans. Walter H. Principe in his *Faith, History and Cultures: Stability and Change in Church Teachings* (Milwaukee, WI: Marquette University Press, 1991), p. 8.

17 See Aquinas's *Summa Theologiae*, Ia, q. 84, a. 7, ad 3.

18 On the Adornoesque *via negativa*, see Julian Roberts, *The Logic of Reflection:German Philosophy in the Twentieth Century* (New Haven and London: Yale University Press, 1992), p. 240.

19 Ibid., p. 242.

20 'Il ne peut y avoir, séparée de la relation avec les hommes, aucune "connaissance" de Dieu': Emmanuel Lévinas, *Totalité et Infini*, 3rd edn (The Hague: Martinus Nijhoff, 1984), p. 51. Schillebeeckx refers to this remark in JWC, p. 57, and III, p. 94.

8

Coming to grips with God

Hegel once wrote that when confronted by a philosophical work that has a substantial, solid content, the easiest procedure one can adopt in response to it is simply to judge it. More taxing is an attempt to grasp it. And most difficult of all is to produce a systematic account of it by combining judging and grasping.[1]

I take his point. In this book I have passed several judgements on Schillebeeckx's theology and its philosophical substratum. I have sought in the first place to evaluate his output according to whether or not he qualifies as an outstanding Christian thinker. In my view, he most assuredly does. However, in the final analysis, I cannot take what was for Hegel the simplest step of making an all-encompassing judgement, for the obvious reason that Schillebeeckx continues to expound his ideas. Hence, any estimations or characterizations of his theology in its current form necessarily need to be partial and reserved. In the preceding pages, I have certainly striven to lay bare my own understanding of his work's content, and to provide an account of its present constitution. Precisely because his writings are so voluminous and multifarious, this book has been construed as a guide to what I perceive as the pillars of his thought.

THE CREATIVE ONENESS OF GOD, JESUS CHRIST AND HUMANITY

To recapitulate and draw our review of Schillebeeckx's life and thought to a close, I should re-emphasize that creation is the master-concept of his output. In this book I have made much of his debt to Aquinas, a debt he accentuated when he declared, not without force, that Aquinas is indeed a source of inspiration for him, although in a way different from those who, as he says, 'choose to divorce themselves from the present-day experience of human existence and its analysis in modern philosophy and lock themselves up in a room with all of Aquinas's works' (RT2, p. 75). Nevertheless, with regard to the way in which Schillebeeckx understands reality as a *unitary* divine creation, he is also considerably indebted to Aquinas's forerunner, Albert the Great. One of Schillebeeckx's predominant theological preoccupations concerns grace: God's presence to humankind. Albert, more so than Aquinas, and according to Schillebeeckx, blurred distinctions between grace and nature:

> For Albert, any phenomenon — and he was a good observer — in nature, in social structures and among human beings, was also God's concern. For him, politics, mysticism, episcopal finances, getting hold of an authentic text of Aristotle, was all an expression of one and the same spirituality. It was from him that Meister Eckhart learnt that it is not the contemplative Mary but the active Martha who is the model of the true mystic. (GAU, p. 226)

In line with Albert, therefore, Schillebeeckx frequently emphasizes that the concerns of human beings are God's concern (JWC, pp. 18 and 28). And like Albert, he can maintain that God's grace is 'not a special realm of inwardness, but the whole reality in which we live and of which we ourselves are a part' (II, p. 812). In short, a distinguishing mark of Schillebeeckx's theology is the resolution with which he describes graced reality as a unitary divine creation in which God, Jesus Christ and humanity are *one*, 'in the sense that they can never be set over against one another or in competition with one another' (JWC, p. 31; III, p. 15). In the third part of his Christological trilogy, Schillebeeckx points out that the oneness of creation includes animals, plants, organic and inorganic creatures, 'for God is not just a God of human beings' (III, p. 236).

ENCOUNTER, HUMANITY, AND NEGATIVITY

Understanding reality as a divine creation, Schillebeeckx has channelled the intellectual passions of his career into an elaboration of the twin and ever-present pillars of his thought: faith in God the Creator-Saviour, and in Jesus of Nazareth, the Condensation of Creation and Manifestation of Salvation. Furthermore, he elaborates the meaning of Christian faith in God and Jesus by relying on three interwoven notions that stand as the conceptual building blocks of his theology: encounter, humanity and negativity. If reference to Albert and Aquinas is an illumination of Schillebeeckx's continuation of Dominican theological traditions, then to concentrate on the three building blocks is to converge on his theological inventiveness and originality.

Let us briefly consider each of the notions in turn as a way of summarily drawing together the threads of Schillebeeckx's writings and especially of his more mature theological thought.

(a) Encounter

From beginning to end, Edward Schillebeeckx's writings are focused on the hoary theological pursuit of explaining *the meaning* of Christian faith's assertion that human beings are able to know and encounter God in the flux of human history. The architectonic question of his theology, therefore, is what I have frequently referred to above as the interchange between universality and particularity. There are many other, more traditional and theological ways of labelling the same interplay: nature–supernature; freedom–grace; God–humanity; and Church–world. To explain faith in a divine-human nexus, Schillebeeckx does not proceed on the footing of an avowedly philosophical speculation. Rather, he falls back on the existentialist notion of intersubjective and interpersonal encounter. For Schillebeeckx, Christian faith asserts that to encounter God one must first encounter Jesus. And Jesus, in turn, is met in a community gathered in his name: the Church. One encounters Jesus, so the argument unfolds, in the sense of acting as he did: by contacting the human refuse of a given society; establishing communication with those excommunicated social outcasts; and practically resisting unjust excommunicators.

Even though the theme of encounter is a strong and pervasive undercurrent throughout Schillebeeckx's publications, there is an important evolution in the way the theme is deployed. The intersubjective encounter of his initial work was explained most notably in a sacramental context and was broached primarily, though not exclusively, in terms of an individual person's contact with God. The encounter in question, then, was conceived as one-to-One; between subject and God. Schillebeeckx's later work expanded the twofold one-to-One schema of his early career into a threefold pattern of a one-to-others-to-One contact. Otherwise expressed, his more recent writings stress to a far greater extent that a person's contact with God is mediated primarily through others: through an encounter with human beings who are gripped in the teeth of misery, and cold-shouldered by their contemporaries. In this later view, therefore, an encounter with Jesus through the Church is not described as the only way for a human being to encounter God.

(b) Humanity

An encounter with vilified persons unavoidably raises the matter of humanity, or rather, their impaired humanity. For Schillebeeckx, that which is human, the *humanum*, is indefinable because it is an eschatological reality: it finds its ultimate meaning in relation to God's absolute transcendence which includes an as yet unknown and literally inconceivable future. 'God is more human than any human being' (GAU, p. 177). So the meaning of humanity points to the God of the Future (GFM). Human beings, in the midst of their sufferings, can at least imagine and hope for a more humane existence. The *humanum*, therefore, is sought not caught. Moreover, Jesus' ultimate identity and relation to God are explicable in relation to both his own humanity and his attempts to humanize the existence of others. To humanize is basically to obliterate injustice. In Schillebeeckx's view, Jesus is human like us, except that he is more human (GAU, p. 115). The Church, with its social function of critical negativity (see p. 128), has the function of perpetuating the humanizing action of Jesus. This aspect of Schillebeeckx's more recent theology is of exceptional consequence: there can be no talk of the meaning of Christian faith in terms of a supposedly pure, asocial, atemporal and ahistorical theory that is disembodied and disengaged from current experiences and day-to-day human practices. What faith might mean, therefore, depends in the first place on how believers express it in their actions. 'Jesus acts as God acts' (JWC, p. 20). Therefore, Christians must act as Jesus acted. Otherwise their professions of faith become vacuous and duplicitous. All of which is summed up in the remark: 'Talk about God always stands under the primacy of praxis' (GAU, p. 99).

According to Edward Schillebeeckx, therefore, human beings are the story of God (III). In other words, their attempts to humanize the dehumanized reflect the very nature of God who is the fullness of humanity. If humans are God's story or fundamental symbol, then Jesus is God's face, so to say: to witness the humanity of Jesus is to glimpse something of God's nature (see FSG, p. 47). And the Church, the community gathered in Jesus' name, may also exhibit the human face of God, to speak metaphorically (CHF).

The significance of the themes of humanity and encountering the dehumanized in Schillebeeckx's theology is captured in a eucharistic prayer that he wrote and included in the epilogue to the second part of his Christological trilogy. Addressed to God, part of the prayer reads as follows:

We remember that
wherever your Jesus came,
people rediscovered their humanity,
and so were filled with new riches,
so that they could give one another
new courage in their lives.

We remember
how he spoke to people,
about a lost coin,
a sheep that had strayed, a lost son:
of all those who are lost and no longer count,
out of sight, out of mind; the weak and the poor,
all those who are captive, unknown, unloved.

We recall that
he went to search for all who were lost,
for those who are saddened and out in the cold,
and how he always took their side,
without forgetting the others.

And that cost him his life,
because the mighty of the earth would not tolerate it.
And yet, good God, almighty Father,
he knew that he was understood and accepted by you,
he saw himself confirmed by you in love.

So he became one with you.
And so, freed from himself,
he could live a life of liberation for others.[2]

(c) Negativity

Schillebeeckx's positive affirmations about God, for example, that God is a Pure Positivity, have been checked or negated during his career in two ways. In the first, he has always insisted that on a conceptual level, 'we as human beings really do not know God' (GAU, p. 43). Thus, at the heart of his theology, negativity is present in the form of apophatism: we know positively only what God is not. In his early works, however, he still suggested that a non-conceptual factor of knowledge, linked with its conceptual opposite, implicitly establishes a cognitive contact with, or theoretical *participation* in, a totality of meaning. The second apophatic checking of his positive affirmations came when he negated the very idea that the knowledge of faith furnishes an implicit intuition of a meaning-totality. His later works, therefore, speak solely of a practical *anticipation* of a totality of meaning, the completeness of which is envisaged in the future. As he observes: 'Religion is about the totality of meaning of our human existence. In every particular experience there is something of an (anticipating) experience of totality.'[3]

A major difference between Schillebeeckx's early and later theology is that the *via negativa* of his early discourses on God came to be applied to his later writings on Jesus, the Church, and humankind. Karl Barth insisted earlier this century that the classical Catholic *via triplex* ought to be replaced by a way of dialectics (*via dialectica*), which compresses the threefold steps of the *via triplex* into two operations of assertion and counter-assertion with regard to propositions concerning God. Schillebeeckx not only retained the *via triplex* with its crucial step of *via negativa* in the context of his discussions concerning God, but, as I have said, he applied it subsequently to Christology, ecclesiology, and anthropology. For instance, whereas his early works spoke of Jesus as a God–man, his later publications insist that God is revealed in a *non-divine* aspect of Jesus' humanity (FSG, p. 108). To accompany an apophatic theology, therefore, Schillebeeckx eventually developed a negative, apophatic Christology; negative in the sense of being less conceptualized. Ironically, by stopping short of interpreting Jesus in the explicitly conceptualist terms of, for example, 'person' and 'nature', Schillebeeckx's later writings are more reverential. Not only do they safeguard a reverence for, or awareness of, God's transcendence, they also refrain from contending that Jesus' identity could be adequately encapsulated by a particular theory, hypothesis or concept.

Moreover, although Schillebeeckx's initial sacramental writings spoke in glowing terms of the Church as a primordial sacrament, his later publications still speak of the Church as a sacrament of God's salvation, but concurrently espouse a negative ecclesiology, or an ecclesiology in a minor key, which points out that the Church is not immune to criticism as if it were a spotless gift from heaven (see III, pp. xv and xix; and JWC, p. 31). Consequently, and to illustrate, Schillebeeckx can now ask of Christians known to him:

> Has not our church again become a fortified temple, almost a new stronghold, from which the prophetic breath has disappeared, where God's praise may indeed be sung but where people are trampled under foot? Has not the fetish of doctrine and the fortified logic of orthodoxy taken the place of the cattle and sheep of Jerusalem, though this time human beings are made sacrificial animals? Do we not need a new cleansing of the temple? (FSG, p. 41)

Once more it could be stressed that an ironical outcome of Schillebeeckx's development of an apophatic ecclesiology is that his theology has become more reverential towards God, for surely, it is just as idolatrous to elevate the Church to an unassailable and absolute status as it is to absolutize or apotheosize a relative thing like a concept or Christological doctrine. In safeguarding God's transcendence in theological reflection, Schillebeeckx excels.

As for the matter of an apophatic anthropology, Schillebeeckx's early writings relied on a philosophical examination of humankind that was cast in the form of the phenomenological categories of Merleau-Ponty and the existential terms of Georges Gusdorf. Hegel spoke of the 'absolute freedom' pertaining to religion, philosophy, and art. Schillebeeckx spoke of God as an 'absolute freedom' and a human being as a 'situated freedom'. In the second volume of his Christological trilogy, however, he outlined an anthropology in a meagre way, by describing humankind in terms of seven 'anthropological constants', or basic determining features of humankind. In his book *Jesus in Our Western Culture*, he underscores that the *humanum* is indefinable. He then suggests in terms of three biblical metaphors what its eschatological fulfilment might entail: 'the kingdom of God'; 'the resurrection of the body'; and 'the new heaven and the new earth' (pp. 29–30).[4]

CONCLUSION

In the light of Schillebeeckx's far-reaching application of the negative way in various subdimensions of his theology, the most important thing he has to teach anyone who is remotely interested in what Christians call 'God' is that in human history, one never comes to grips with God. Schillebeeckx's thought is decidedly doxological in its deference to God's transcendence. While human history is in progress, the most those who seek God can do is to struggle to point in God's direction. There is no religion, Church, person, theory, praxis, or concept that circumscribes the plenitude of the God proclaimed by Christian faith, for only God is absolute. And yet, to say that God is inaccessible and indefinable is not to report an atheistic, anti-ecclesiastical failure to praise God: it is one form such praise can assume.

According to Schillebeeckx, faith is a struggle: ' "to believe in God" is to wrestle with God, as Jacob/Israel once wrestled with God's angel' (III, p. 63). By his own account he has been struggling and trying to come to grips with God throughout his life. He recently described himself as 'a theologian who all his life did nothing but seek what God can mean for men and women, tentatively and stammeringly' (III, p. xv). Coming to grips with Schillebeeckx, I would propose, is to approach an able guide in the enterprise of searching for, understanding something of, and trying to come to grips with God, however falteringly. Schillebeeckx is outstanding, it seems to me, in pointing out that the cardinal rule of a religious life, that is, a life spent seeking God, is not a matter of finding or adequately comprehending God (see FSG, p. 85). Rather, the dominant principle governing an endeavour to search for God is just that: to search.

Notes

1   See G. W. F. Hegel, whom I have loosely paraphrased here, in *The Phenomenology of Mind*, trans. J. B. Baillie (New York: Harper & Row, 1967), pp. 69–70.
2   II, pp. 848–9. In the third line of the passage just quoted, I exchanged the word 'men' in the English translation for 'people', which renders just as adequately the Dutch original's use of the term *mensen*.
3   Edward Schillebeeckx, 'Religion of and for men: towards a criteriology of religion and religiosity', *Sevartham* (1979), pp. 3–20 (p. 7).
4   These three visions were sketched previously in Edward Schillebeeckx, 'Christelijke spiritualiteit als ziel en bevrijding van de ethiek', *Tijdschrift voor Geestelijk Leven* 41 (1985), pp. 407–18 (pp. 416–18).

Index